COMMAND YOUR WORLD

Ten Communication Strategies to Present your Best Self and Win

Dr. Bonnie Winfrey

All rights reserved. No part of this publication may be reproduced, distributed, or transmitted in any form or by any means, including photocopying, recording, or other electronic or mechanical methods, without the prior written permission of the author. Permission requests should be addressed to "Attention: Permissions Coordinator," and emailed to the address below.

All quotes, unless otherwise noted, are from the New King James Version. Copyright 1979, 1980, 1982 by Thomas Nelson, Inc. Used by permission. All rights reserved. Scriptures marked KJV are taken from The Holy Bible, King James Version. Public Domain. Holy Bible, New Living Translation, copyright ©1996, 2004, 2015 by Tyndale House Foundation. Used by permission of Tyndale House Publishers Inc., Carol Stream, Illinois 60188. All rights reserved. Holy Bible, New International Version®, NIV®Copyright ©1973, 1978, 1984, 2011 by Biblica, Inc.® All rights reserved worldwide.

ISBN: 978-1-7373707-2-7

Copyright © 2022 Bonnie Winfrey

www.bonniewinfrey.com
info@bonniewinfrey.com
815-744-5340
Cover Design by Caio Almeida Graphics: Ronnie Voss & Aspire Design + Brand
Typsetting by Becky English of Aspire Design + Brand

Printed in the USA

Endorsements

Bonnie is on point in *Command Your World*. She has a unique ability to analyze issues and promptly develop strategies that are concise, no nonsense, and provide solid direction on how to win.

I worked with Bonnie at WLS, the ABC station in Chicago early in our careers. In a sea of "A" personalities, she stood out as a calm, efficient and steady force. In the midst of chaos, she was searching for solutions!

The strategies presented in this book exemplify Bonnie's kind, but direct approach, which is refreshing in a world of mixed messages through the manipulation of semantics.

Bonnie is trustworthy and reliable, and those qualities shine through. Her writing shows the level of knowledge and experience you want to guide you along your professional journey.

Diann Burns
TV News Anchor
9 time Emmy Award Winner
ABC, NBC, CBS

The United States medical system is the most technologically advanced in the world, yet medical error is a leading cause of preventable death in the country. The most common root cause of medical error is communication failure. Additionally, what has emerged as a major contributor to increased risks for medical error is burn out and loss of joy.

Bonnie has presented strategies that are urgently needed in patient and care team safety. The strategies presented in this book should be implemented in any setting where effective communication is required. Everyone working in safety-critical settings will greatly benefit from this book, especially those of us who work in health care settings.

Ron Wyatt, MD
Institute for Healthcare Improvement
Healthcare Improvement Fellow and former Patient Safety Officer,
The Joint Commission

To see Bonnie Winfrey in action and on stage is to observe the height of effective communication. I have been twice-honored to be a co-presenter with Bonnie on the topic of communication. Now, this brilliant and beautiful woman is sharing her wise and deep reflection on strategies to master and polish communication for anyone in every walk of life and in any circumstance. I have found there is no feeling like any other when connecting persuasively with an audience, whether of one person or a thousand. Bonnie's command of communication is positive, remarkably practical, and completely at ease in all its forms.

As I read her words, I could hear her voice in my mind's ear, almost as if I once again was sitting in rapt attention. As a manager and community leader, expert communication was essential for my success. I have found that I am in better control from what I have learned from Bonnie. Now her sage advice is available for everyone's benefit. As Bonnie writes, "Imagine the world as one huge stage. . . called Life." Optimize your role in life; make the decision to learn from Bonnie's communication strategies and "command your world."

Randy Chapman
Former Publisher, The Herald News, Joliet, IL
Publisher Emeritus, Post-Bulletin Co., Rochester, MN

Daily, I speak with business owners and aspiring entrepreneurs about starting and scaling their businesses. Statistics show that one of the primary reasons a company may fail is the owner or sales team's inability to communicate their unique selling proposition, which means they have difficulty explaining why customers should choose their service or product. While this example speaks to the importance of communication in business, communication is essential to success in every area of life.

Command Your World is a must-read for anyone looking to become the best you. Bonnie is a consummate professional and anointed to help you take your relationships, career, business, and dreams to the next level. While providing necessary techniques, her approach also includes who a person at their core is in the development process.

Melissa Duff Brown
Director of Strategy
Joseph Business Services & All Related Entities

For most people the ability to communicate well is an acquired skill. Mastering the skill of effective communication is like possessing a passport at the border crossing between failure and success. As a judge and former trial lawyer, I know this to be true. In this book, Bonnie Winfrey provides thoughtful and useful insights on the nature, methodology, and fruit of effective communication.

Judge Vincent F. Cornelius
Past President, Illinois State Bar Association
Past Chancellor, Academy of Illinois lawyers

Bonnie was sent from above! When I first met Bonnie I had failed several interviews, lacked the confidence to speak in front of people, and felt like giving up — I was stuck. Bonnie was able to assess my need and provide personalized coaching and "therapy" that transformed me from the inside out. I learned practical communication skills and practiced techniques with Bonnie. Soon after rounds of coaching with Bonnie, I had a series of speaking engagements and I nailed each one of them and I finally passed an arduous interview, too. Thanks to Bonnie, I was able to accomplish what I previously thought was impossible. She helped me break down the barriers to effective communication and I now have more confidence and better connections with people. Bonnie, you have changed my life! Thank you!

I would encourage anyone who is feeling stuck or ready for the next level in their communication skills to read this book and consider consulting with Bonnie for individualized coaching. You will see results!

Dr. Patrina Singleton
NBCT Chicago Public School Principal

Congratulations on completing your work on effective communication! It is easy to read, great examples and I love how you challenge the reader. This book will help anyone wanting to improve their communication skills and I look forward to sharing with my leadership team!

Carolyn D. Seward
President/Chief Executive Officer
Family and Workforce Centers of America
St. Louis, MO

I'm happy to offer my enthusiastic endorsement of the coaching in corporate communications I have received from Bonnie. She is nothing short of brilliant! As an emergency medicine physician for over thirty years, I am acutely aware of how crucial well-timed coaching on very specific issues can be.

Bonnie Winfrey has the ability to perceive the dynamics of an individual in their workplace in such a way as to be a guide for both growth and defense. I have come away with an enhanced sense of self and new appreciation of the non-technical factors in my work as a physician. The "people stuff " is something very different than what we learn in school and hospital training. Both business and leadership are areas that are missing in much of medical curriculum. Bonnie is a lifesaver.

B. Ellen Wesley, DO
Emergency Medicine Physician

Bonnie Winfrey's easy to read, absorb, and understand book, *Command Your World*, is simply unique and beautifully written. It takes you on a pleasant journey that keeps you focused on learning the ten strategies which will indeed help you polish and master effective communication skills. She highlights key strategies and makes impressive sense of the increasingly important role of good communication in our world.

King Solomon in Proverbs 15:2 (NIV) puts it quite simply; "The tongue of the wise adorns knowledge but the mouth of the fool gushes folly." Bonnie who has trained thousands of people in the area of communication, humbly and joyfully accepts herself as an instrument used by God to impart her gifted communication skills to others. This book, Command Your World reflects the gift of God as she communicates over 30 years of varied experience as a former newspaper reporter, and acknowledged and award-winning producer and director.

I would encourage you to purchase this book, Command Your World. As an adjunct professor, I recommend this book to all my MBA students as a resource library and ensure it gets in the hands of my business colleagues. Bonnie has created an important resource, a must-read for superior communication!!!

Chief Jimmy G. Delano
Founder of Harmony International Group

Bonnie is truly a blessed woman of God and a joy to meet. She is smart, intelligent and is an example of success possibilities. Bonnie is dynamic, spiritual, and an inspiration to all she comes in contact with. She has spent her life's work helping others to be more successful in their lives. I am certain that this book will challenge, inspire, educate and help those who read it put into action the steps and strategies outlined in her work.

Dr. Barbara Young
Author, Entrepreneur, Coach, TV/Radio Personality

Congratulations! *Command Your World* is an excellent book for anyone who desires to improve their communication skills. I was not surprised reading the book, because Bonnie Winfrey is the consummate communicator! Command Your World would be a great addition to your library.

Dr. Jawanza Kunjufu
Best-selling author of over 40 books.

Utilizing Bonnie's expertise over the years as a personal communications coach and now reading her book *Command Your World* certainly has changed my view on communication and changed my life in so many wonderful ways. This book offers a wealth of information and knowledge in the importance of communication. As a person where English is a second language, I have come to understand that communication is a core part of the human experience. The tools contained in this book will help you greatly improve your listening and speaking skills and provides the platform and "how to's" for reaching your full potential. I recommend this book to anyone who has a strong desire for personal growth and improvement as well as monetary results.

Dr. Emmy Wang, DC
Owner of Advanced Wellness Center / Chiropractic Physician

Foreward

How are you doing when it comes to effective communication? When you interact one-on-one with someone important in your life, is it a highly enjoyable experience for both of you? When you lead a meeting or attend a group function, are others inspired to follow your instructions and take action? When you speak to an audience, are you confident enough to command the room regardless of what happens during your speech? If you can't answer these questions with a resounding yes, then you need to learn how to improve your communication. In *Command Your World*, Dr. Bonnie Winfrey has outlined ten communication strategies that will help you to present your best self in all forms of communication.

Whether you are an introvert or an extrovert there are life-changing strategies in this book that can help you take your communication skills to the next level. As a corporate executive, I learned early in my career that it wasn't so much about how much I knew but more about how well I could communicate with others through verbal and non-verbal skills.

In this powerful book, Dr. Winfrey takes you through an experience that is not often found in professional publications. She starts with an intra-evaluation that allows the reader to examine the root cause of self-doubt and unproductive thinking that hinders effective communication. Then she takes the reader on a journey of preparation in section two of the book where practical and easy to learn communication strategies are provided. The third section of this book is for sure my favorite! In it Dr. Winfrey provides strategies on how to enjoy your new-found confidence and skills by showing up on stages as your best self.

One thing I know for sure is that those who communicate well take their relationships, their work, and their lives to higher heights. I can boldly make this statement because it happened for me. By applying the communication tools outlined in this book, I enjoy speaking on stages around the globe, leading a successfully training, coaching, and speaking business and hosting a top-rated global television broadcast. It can happen for you too. Even if communicating with others isn't something you're good at today, you can learn how to do it and become better by applying the ten communication strategies in this book.

Why should you learn how to communicate better? Because regardless of your purpose, vocation, gender, race, or national origin, effective communication is the foundation to your success as it touches every aspect of your life. Author and psychotherapist, Virginia Satir said it best when she said, "Communication is to a relationship what breathing is to maintaining life."

Why should you read this book? Because Dr. Winfrey is an encourager and she not only provides the most effective communication strategies on the market today, but she provides a breath to business and personal communication that increases the stability of an enjoyable life. Throughout the book, Bonnie encourages the practice of self- realization through affirmation. She shares the secrets and techniques taught to her private coaching clients and that alone is priceless.

Dr. Winfrey and I met early in our careers while working at Cable News Network (CNN) in Atlanta, GA. She was a powerful speaker even back then, and today she is a phenomenal communicator, coach, and businesswoman who has mastered setting her stage, owning her stage, and enjoying her stage. But it didn't come easy for Bonnie. Like many of us, she had obstacles to overcome. She shares her personal story of overcoming trials and tribulations. Undoubtedly one of the things that fuels her passion for helping others to become overcomers through effective communication.

I have eagerly awaited the release of this book which outlines many of the communication tools Dr. Winfrey has shared with me over the years. This body of work has not only met my exceptions but exceeded them. I wholeheartedly recommend *Command Your World* by Dr. Bonnie Winfrey and will be sharing the strategies outlined in this book with my corporate training clients. If you want to learn how to communicate more effectively and thereby command your world, this book is for you. I strongly believe—regardless of age, experience, or natural ability—that the ten strategies in this book will help you to become a stronger communicator.

Dr. Yvette Gavin
International Speaker, TV Host of Faith at Work,
Chief Learning Officer at Yvette Gavin Consulting,
SUCCESS Magazine's 125 Leaders to Know in 2022

Dedication

I dedicate this book to God for giving me the gift to communicate, teach, and transform lives. *Command Your World* was born out of a request by Corporate America asking me to write a book.

For everyone who has a desire to master your destiny and propel your communication skills to new heights, this book is for you.

I further dedicate this book to my loving husband of thirty-seven years, Keith, and our two wonderful sons, Kailen and Kyler. They are my WHY. I thank them for being supportive during this fantastic journey.

Acknowledgements

Life is a winding road we all travel, and I was blessed to have a godly beginning that strengthened and prepared me for each twist and turn. I sincerely thank my parents, the late Levi and Loucreasie Williams, for their nurturing love and support. I thank my father for living outside the box, being a true entrepreneur and for teaching me how nothing is impossible. I thank my mother for being a woman of great substance, demanding the same from me and for directing me into the career I embrace today.

I also want to thank the late Dr. Pearl Singleton, a very special lady, who from the day my mother transitioned into eternity, stepped into her shoes and nurtured me into the life I live today. Further appreciation also goes to her husband my former pastor, Dr. Isaac Singleton of Mt. Zion Baptist Church of Joliet, Illinois. He taught me and encouraged me to use my gifts and dream big!

I started this book under Dr. Singleton, but I must also give thanks to God for directing my family to our present pastor, Dr. Bill Winston of Living Word Christian Center in Forest Park, Illinois. He gave me the motivation I needed to finish this book. I can't thank Pastor Winston enough for his profound wisdom and teachings.

I extend sincere gratitude to my sisters and brother who encourage and support me.

I also want to thank one of my former clients, the Joint Commission, for it was in training Joint Commission surveyors that I was given the opportunity to take my communications training to a higher level. I have trained thousands of people in the area of communications and a good portion of that number have been Joint Commission surveyors from across the country.

I am grateful to the following people who have assisted me in pulling my book together: My team of editors; Becky English of Aspire Design & Brand for layout and design, as well as these profound thought leaders who kept me focused: Cynthia Krohn, Yvette Gavin, LaTonya Burton, Dr. Tanjie Brewer, Dr. Deborah Smith Pegues, Dr. Keith Winfrey and Dr. Barbara Young.

Contents

Introduction

COMMUNICATION   16
Your Key to Opening a New World of Understanding

PART I — Set Your Stage   36
Strategy 1   Know Yourself
Strategy 2   Know Your Neighbor
Strategy 3   Know Your Enemy

PART II — Own Your Stage   88
Strategy 4   Prepare Yourself
Strategy 5   Prepare Your Materials
Strategy 6   Understand Your Environment
Strategy 7   Know Your Audience
Strategy 8   Engage Your Audience

PART III — Enjoy Your Stage   166
Strategy 9   Enjoy Yourself
Strategy 10   Let Your Body Speak

COMMUNICATION CLINIC   192

Introduction

Welcome to Command Your World!

Within these pages lies a wealth of valuable knowledge for personal and professional development in the area of communications. Through practical scenarios, you will get simple solutions to everyday communication challenges and learn how to improve your ability to handle negative communication issues.

The theories and solutions expressed in this book have been proven many times. They have helped thousands of business executives, administrators, medical personnel, and students reach new heights in their interactions with others and in their corporate, private, and personal lives.

I designed this communication book, Command Your World, to help you polish and master effective communication skills. The ten strategies outlined in this book will help you identify and diagnose negative communication, offer treatment options, and ultimately teach you how to communicate successfully in all areas of your life.

For ease in absorbing and digesting it all, I have organized the book into three parts:
- **Part I**: Set Your Stage
- **Part II**: Own Your Stage
- **Part III**: Enjoy Your Stage

While all of these parts are packed full of helpful information for any form of communication, **Part I** is about self-development, healing, and restoration. **Part II** is specifically focused on prepping and planning for public speaking engagements. **Part III** discusses transformation and offers insight, tools, and wisdom on how to communicate effectively with various audiences and individuals.

I urge you to digest one strategy at a time. At the end of each section, you will be presented with a "Challenge." This is your opportunity to reflect on what you have read and think about new ways to apply the strategies outlined in each chapter. Also, as I am a firm believer in the power of the spoken word, I have included a "Declaration" at the end of each section for you to speak out loud to yourself. State it daily and tap into the creative power you hold in your tongue!

Are you ready? Let's get started!

COMMUNICATION

*Your Key to Opening
A New World of Understanding*

Try to imagine a world *without* communication. Many experts claim that communication doesn't exist when people stop speaking to each other verbally. Some say communication ceases when battle lines are drawn in wars, and the opposing sides shut down contact. Still, others say communication is impossible between individuals who don't speak the same language, claiming that they experience disconnection because they cannot conduct verbal communication.

I beg to differ with experts who make these claims. Communication never ceases. If you go shopping at a grocery store and keep to yourself, there is still communication. A newborn who is unable to speak communicates. People who are unable to hear, see, or speak communicate all the time.

Likewise, many believe that communication is complicated, but I say it is simple. Consider, for example, a healthy man in his fifties who is suddenly stricken with a deadly diagnosis of meningitis. His doctors inform his family that his survival looks grim. Yet, his ninety-year-old mother, refusing to accept the prognosis, walks into her son's hospital room. Her son is unable to speak or move but finds the strength to turn his head and raise one finger. His mother responds by touching her index finger to his. From the patient's eye drops a tear. A smile emerges on the mother's face. That is simple communication.

More than fifteen years after saying, "I do" to commitment and to their dreams, a married couple wakes up one day and finds they hardly have a word to say to each other. That's communication.

There are various ways to communicate.

- A young teenager, confused about the world in which he lives, decides to run away, leaving behind frustrated parents. That's communication.
- The son who yearns to be understood by his father who discounts his feelings is still communicating.
- The alcoholic who lives to die as he looks to the end of every bottle for hope and fulfillment is communicating.
- The young child who constantly rebels against authority is communicating.
- The forces of nature also communicate in inexplicable variations of weather. Flowers that bloom in the spring and bring beauty into our lives also communicate a message.

These messages prove to us every day that communication is alive and well.

Communication Methods

We communicate in three ways: through words, through our body language, and through our spirit. We will explore all three of these throughout this book, but first, let's briefly introduce them:

We Communicate through Our Words

Words, whether spoken or written, are powerful. They can make us feel good, hurt us, build us up, or tear us down. They can make us feel pretty or handsome, accepted or unaccepted. They can inspire peace or incite mass chaos and destruction.

We Communicate through Our Bodies

Nonverbal cues can communicate love, happiness, and joy, and they can also communicate fear or hate. Our body language can reveal the truth behind a lying tongue. Inappropriate body language can inflict pain that feels like an emotional knife to the heart.

We Communicate through Our Spirits

Our spirits communicate happiness, sadness, good, evil, right, wrong, hate, and love. Our spirits can defeat us or be used to defeat others. The spirit of your business, organization, church, or home can be interpreted as positive or negative. In turn, the positive or negative spirit of a person can infiltrate an environment and influence it either positively or negatively.

Imagine the world as one huge stage. The stage is set, and the curtain goes up. The scene is called **Life**. What part are you playing? There are seven cultural mountains that influence each of us and our society - arts and entertainment, business, education, government, family, media, and religion. The goal of this dominion should be to possess at least one mountain, master the influence, and create a positive world. What's the key? **Communication!**

The goal of this dominion should be to possess at least one mountain, master the influence, and create a positive world. The key? Communication!

Foundations of Communication

Before we walk through each strategy, let's look at some foundations of communication:

- Communication is powerful.

- Communication requires etiquette.
- Communication must be effective.
- Communication requires focus.
- Communication requires trust.
- Communication requires information.

Communication Is Powerful

Understand the art of the interview. There is a profound desire among humans to know the unknown, an insatiable curiosity that can drive us to do and say things we might never have considered before someone spoke it into our ear. I'm not referring to senseless, mindless babble, but the deliberate pursuit or dissemination of information. Such communication is what I call an interview. In fact, the world as we know it today was redesigned through an interview. A conversation between Eve and a serpent changed God's vision for His children and their world forever. Genesis 3 explains how God clearly communicated to Adam about the trees he could eat from the Garden of Eden, and it was all but one.

A crafty serpent managed to place doubt in Eve's mind by telling her God was trying to keep something from them. He told Eve if she ate of the forbidden tree, she and Adam would be as gods, knowing good and evil. The serpent convinced Eve through clever phrasing and suggestions, and she fell for his scheme. She ate the forbidden fruit, and the Bible says she gave unto her husband and he also ate the fruit.

This interview, this exchange of information—this casual conversation—shows the power of communication. The action taken by Adam and Eve through this dialogue forced all mankind into a lifetime of hardship and separated us from communicating easily with our Creator and with each other. The same curiosity that prompted Eve to make that fateful decision also dwells in us; we hold the power to sway or be swayed. Though we don't always recognize it, we practice the art of the interview every day. Any time we communicate with someone, we are involved in an interview process, even if it's just a casual conversation.

Interviewing is not just something we do to get a job. Interviewing is comprised of an exchange of verbal and/or nonverbal messages. The multifaceted nature of interviewing plays a big part in our lives, and it infuses our culture more than we think:

- A salesman persuading a customer.
- A teacher working through a problem with a student.
- A reporter questioning an eyewitness about a neighborhood robbery.
- A manager training a new employee on how to perform a job and checking to be sure she understands.
- A supervisor reprimanding an employee about an infraction.
- An administrator asking a patient about his stay in the hospital.

Each of these situations are interviews. An interview is simply planned communication. It does not come naturally; it is a learned process, and we will examine that more closely next..

Communication Requires Etiquette

The old adage, "He who fails to plan, plans to fail," holds true in the realm of interviewing. Many physicians have attended higher-learning institutions for advanced medical training programs and learned about medical breakthroughs and evidence-based care, but later found they lacked the communication skills needed to connect with patients.

I remember one particular doctor's visit. In the exam room, he told me all my test results were normal and ended with, "I'll see you in six months." Leaving the room, he added, "Oh, by the way, one test did reveal you have a little acid reflux, but don't worry about it." By the time he mentioned this added information, the door was open, and he was heading into the next patient's exam room. I immediately asked him nicely to come back and talk to me. I felt I deserved his attention and the privacy to learn more about the condition.

Medical schools across the country are working to solve this problem by integrating curriculums involving communication training. Business executives are hiring communication companies to train their personnel. Why? Communication etiquette is a learned process. The Japanese were one of the first to grasp this concept and integrate this etiquette into their curriculum. They uncovered a huge secret: professionally trained employees (in the area of communicating) had a noticeable edge over companies with untrained employees.

Communication etiquette is essential for interacting in today's business arena. Good communication skills usually help in the formation of solid working relationships. Human resource professionals estimate that more than eighty percent of the people who fail at their jobs, do so for one reason: they don't relate well to people.

Successful business people understand that effective communication is a must in today's world of pleasing the customer. Well-developed communication builds relationships with customers and among co-workers and plays an important role in customer and job satisfaction.

Communication Must Be Effective

Learn the process of the interview. It is common for those who feel they are weak at communicating to escape by pursuing employment in technical fields where they can hide behind a computer or other equipment that doesn't require person-to-person interaction. Unfortunately for them, there is no escaping the human element, no matter what field one pursues.

So, how do we communicate effectively? Since interviewing is a learned process and it comprises the vast majority of our communication, we must look at what's involved in the process. While all of the chapters in this book address various elements of the interview process, here are three main elements to keep in mind.

Atmosphere

When interviewing, it is vital to be aware of the conditions around you—the atmosphere. If the room is too hot, your communication can be altered. The same holds true if the room is too cold. The way the seats are positioned plays a major role in effectiveness. The people in the room add to the tone of the interview. If there is someone who is not there but should be, this plays a role as well.

Topic

Another important aspect of interviewing is to develop the information or material you want to discuss. Decide upon your purpose for interviewing an individual or group prior to meeting. Once you decide who you're talking to and the purpose, organize your interview questions and set them up in some logical manner, so you're not bouncing from subject to subject.

Comfort

Comfort also plays a role in any effective interview. If you are away from your surroundings, you are a guest on someone else's turf. If you are on your own ground, it is important to help the interviewee feel comfortable. There should be a willingness on the part of the people communicating (both sides) to reveal and exchange information. When interviewees feel they are being treated fairly, what usually follows is a willingness to answer questions honestly.

Communication Requires Focus: Eye Contact and Perception

Focus is vital to a productive and successful interview. Here are three ways to maintain your focus.

Focus by Maintaining Eye Contact

Avoiding eye contact is one of the biggest sins in communication, and shyness is not an excuse for this behavior. If this is hard for you, focus your attention at eye level on the upper bridge of the other person's nose. This makes it feel as if you are looking at the person directly in the eye but doesn't feel uncomfortable for you. Remember, a direct and sincere look will give you confidence and make the other person feel important and heard. The eyes play a critical role in nonverbal communication. The eyes are said to be the window to your soul. They tell your interviewee what he or she needs to know—or even what they don't want to know about you. If your eyes waiver, they can convict you. If they are dancing, they may imply humor or conflict.

Poor eye contact can also change the course of communication. It's difficult to talk to someone who does not look at you. It's also hard to communicate with someone who doesn't consider you important enough to give you their full attention. The eyes are an important tool when communicating. If they are focused in an inappropriate area on an individual, this too can spark negative reactions. A good solution would be to refrain from staring at a person's facial scar or an exposed body part because it can cause discomfort.

A person's eyes reflect emotions such as happiness, sadness and even fear. Along with our eyes, our eyebrows also communicate messages. When they are positioned up, it conveys a message of deep thought, surprise, or disbelief. When they are pulled down and squinted, the message may be confusion or anger. Learn to use eye contact properly when interviewing, and you will see amazing results.

Focus by Controlling Your Perception

There is one word in the English language that can alter or destroy any form of communication: perception. We all have it; some call it radar. It is how we perceive an environment, a person, an attitude. No matter the reality of the case or situation, perception can change and communicate a message. A perception can be formed from a person's action in a particular situation. Action speaks louder than words, no matter how subtle or obvious the nonverbal communication.

> **There is one word in the English language that can alter or destroy any form of communication: *perception.***

Let's take a look at how perception controls our thoughts. Below I have listed some images. Be honest and write your initial perceptions of either positive or negative after each image below.

- A ninety-year-old man wearing hot pants.

  _____

- A 400-pound belly dancer.

  _____

- Trash on the floor of a hospital.

  _____

- A pregnant woman smoking.

  _____

- A person slouched in a chair.

  _____

- A person with dirty fingernails working in a restaurant.

  _____

- An offensive odor in a restaurant.

  _____

- A nurse taking blood without gloves.

  _____

- A priest leaving a casino.

  _____

- A job applicant walking out in the middle of an interview.

  _____

Most, if not all, of these images prompted negative reactions. What makes us react to things or situations? How do we identify something as "abnormal"? Why do we look at the differences in other cultures as being strange? We all have perceptions, and are conditioned by our past and the way we were raised. The real question is, how do we communicate with people in our society who have broken "the rules" of what we perceive as proper etiquette or acceptable? Have the rules really been broken, or is the situation classified negative because it is something unfamiliar to us or something we just don't accept as normal?
No matter what the case may be, controlling perception can help you make progress while communicating. We should look at perception as the third party in a two-person interview. It's always there.

A person's age, sex, race, hair, or weight may communicate a message about an individual or his or her values. The way a person dresses also communicates a message. That message may be positive or negative. What if the CEO of a corporation walked into a business meeting with jeans that had a hole in the knee, and it was not dress-down day? More than likely, the perception would be negative. The unexpected appearance might communicate a message about the CEO of sloppy work habits or negative showmanship.

Perception can also arise when we examine how one sits. Bad posture in a chair can be perceived as laziness, fatigue, or boredom. A person yawning can also send a message of boredom. On the other hand, the person may be suffering from a side effect of medication or could simply be tired and cannot help but yawn.

How Can I Begin Powerfully? Make the decision to be powerful in your approach. Everyone meets new people, but what goes through your mind when you meet someone for the very first time? Usually, you reach out to shake hands. If their shake is weak and limp, what's your response? A handshake creates instant impressions, good or bad. Usually, a weak or limp handshake creates a perception that the person can't be trusted or they are timid, have something to hide, or are insecure. This situation can also be influenced by culture, which is explained further in **Strategy 7, Know Your Audience.**

One day while in a restaurant, I went over to shake hands with a very prominent leader in my community. I was shocked to experience her weak handshake. I'd always had a great deal of respect for this individual but felt something wasn't right. From this regrettable and unforgettable handshake, I learned this person lacked confidence. In her case, it would have been wiser for her to show increased confidence by offering a firm handshake until she naturally increased her confidence on the inside.

An appropriate handshake involves gripping the fingers of another person with an acceptable firmness. A harder handshake does not give you more control. As a matter of fact, if you squeeze too hard, the other person usually perceives negativity. A handshake should be comfortable, not too hard or too soft.

Focus by Handling Toxic People

A conflict can test your ability to stay the course. When navigating in murky waters, anticipate conflict, so you can focus on the outcome of the conversation instead of the battle. You don't have to do one single thing to bring conflict into the communication flow. Some people thrive on it, and some people actually set you up for it. Others simply want to know if you will crumble when confronted by it.

So what happens when conflict arises? How do you handle it? Some people try to wish it away. Some people get involved in it by responding aggressively to the person causing the conflict. Some people ignore it completely. Some fall apart, run from the conflict, and avoid further communication.

The proper way to handle conflict is to remain calm and try to resolve it diplomatically. Keep in mind, in this wonderful world we live in; there are people who are just plain negative. Toxic, negative people live to make others miserable. When confronted with this type of person and their issues, do not show weakness. Try to regain control of the conversation, and don't take the irate person's comments personally. If you do, he or she has won. Stay above the negativity; acknowledge it for what it is, but don't be consumed by it.

Scenario: Jennifer, RN

As a good surgical nurse, Jennifer is given the opportunity to represent and speak on behalf of surgical nurses in her region to express their concerns for more help to a team of administrators and physicians. In a soft voice, she begins by thanking the team for meeting with her and proceeds to communicate concerns compiled by her peers. During her presentation, a physician boisterously states that the requests are unnecessary and he doesn't see the purpose for the meeting. Jennifer, who is already nervous, looks down at the floor and is unable to speak. After a few moments, she tries to continue, but the physician interrupts again and further distracts her by saying her requests are "a bunch of hogwash" and he doesn't want to hear anything else.

Once again, she tries to ignore him, but at this point, the other administrators and physicians are aware of what is going on, and some snicker at the situation. Embarrassed, Jennifer says she will call another meeting at a later date and hastily leaves the room.

This scenario and others like it are real. Every day in similar situations, people like Jennifer are disrespected. What went wrong? It was more than just a rude interruption; Jennifer's response also played a part. Jennifer has always hated conflict. Her father was verbally abusive and always used an irate and boisterous tone to keep her under control. What does this have to do with her speaking to other professionals? As you read further in this book, you will see how childhood experiences, both negative and positive, play a major role in how we function as communicators.

Each of us have assets in our communication arsenal to help control every situation we encounter. Jennifer is no exception. She could have handled the meeting more effectively by exercising techniques unique to her.

Ignoring a conflict is not the answer. Neither was yielding to those who thought less of her because she was not at their professional level. Let's explore some simple solutions.

The right response(s) to a potential heckler would be:

1. Remain calm (displaying smooth and consistent nonverbal communication with her facial and physical demeanor)

2. Acknowledge the heckler (identifying him by name and answering or deferring his question)

3. Recognize the situation for what it is, and

4. Let the physician know that *she* was in charge of the meeting

Jennifer could have responded, "Dr. Phillips, I am interested in your questions and comments, but I would appreciate it if you will let me continue with the rest of my presentation. When I am finished, I will be delighted to discuss your comments."

By integrating this strong message with a firm voice quality (slightly louder - without anger) and appropriate gestures, Dr. Phillips would have clearly recognized Jennifer's confidence and that she was serious about her agenda and wanted to remain in control of the meeting. As a result, Jennifer would have defused the heckler, managed the conflict, and remained on course.

The key word to consider is *manage*. Sometimes we can manage conflict without even speaking. It depends on the individual. A negative conflict can often be managed if you let people know that you are not working against them but are working to improve a situation or help them reach a goal.

Also, be aware of traps set to make you fall prey to conflict. Unfortunately, we live in a society where people desire to take every opportunity to hurt others. Plan for it! Identify and map your way through potential plots. The safest target is a moving target and one that anticipates and handles surprises.

Communication Requires Trust

A prerequisite to successful interviewing involves trust. This attribute of communication doesn't need much explanation. Once trust is broken, the credibility of the person (or organization) becomes tarnished. When this happens, there is little honesty perceived in the interview process, and communication quickly comes to a halt.

Scenario: The Cheating Manager

You are with a manager reading some documentation and excuse yourself to go fill your coffee cup in another room. Upon your return, you notice vital information has been eliminated or changed. Do you ignore what just happened? Do you investigate the matter and ask questions about what is missing? Do you remain quiet and observe what happens farther down the line? How one responds to a situation like this reveals much about their character. How would you respond? Great value is placed on trust in communication.

Communication Requires Information and Asking Questions the Right Way

What kinds of questions are appropriate during the interview process? Questions provide structure and give a foundation to the interview process. There are two approaches to asking questions in the interview process—close-ended and open-ended.

Below are close-ended questions that set the stage for short, direct answers:
Interviewer: "Who is the CEO of this hospital?"
Interviewee: "John Banks."
Interviewer: "Can you tell me where his office is located?"
Interviewee: "Follow me, it's around the corner."
Interviewer: "You sure know your way around here. Did it take a while to learn this maze?"

To stimulate more discussion during an interview, ask open-ended questions:
Interviewer: "Tell me about your CEO and where I can find him?"
Interviewee: "John Banks? He's a wonderful guy, who runs a smooth ship. His office is just right around the corner, but this hospital is a maze. I'll take you there. When I started here, it took me forever to learn my way around."
Interviewer: "I certainly understand."

Which approach gives you the most information? Well, if you are looking for few details and vague answers, the close-ended approach is best. But if you are searching for more conversational feedback, the open-ended approach will provide more. This process also allows the interviewee to express an opinion.

Asking questions is an art in itself, so here are some quick tips. Craft sound questions so the responding individual understands what you are asking. Ask only one question at a time. If you ask two or three questions together, it's difficult to determine which question to answer first—the first one mentioned or the last one asked. When you ask multiple questions at once, you are likely to receive an unanticipated response. For example: "Isn't it a beautiful day today? Are you going to the baseball game? Who's playing? Is Tina going with you? What time does it start?" could result in a response similar to "Yes, the Cubs are playing today." The "yes" could be for the beautiful day or that the person is going and possibly taking Tina. The questions about start time and whether he was going and with whom were not addressed at all.

The human brain responds best to simplicity. When individuals are given too much information to process, they will simply answer the question they remembered. Throwing questions out without thought will result in a response given the same way.

Of course, a better way to pose the questions would have been to ask one question at a time or two at the most. It's easier for the brain to compute answers for two questions and not blow a fuse from overloading it.

Controlling Communication

Can we control the way we communicate? With help, the answer is yes. That's why I wrote Command Your World. God gave us His Ten Commandments as guidelines on how to live on earth. God has given me these ten strategies to help people learn how to communicate more effectively. Learned behaviors from our past, and even our present patterns and habits, can be changed. The ten strategies outlined in this book are designed to help polish communication skills, diagnose negative communication, and offer treatment options as well as improve your ability to communicate effectively.

I strongly believe communication is the key that opens a new world of understanding, and that understanding starts with you. To understand the world around you, you must define yourself. What are your strengths and weaknesses? They play a part in making you a better communicator. Are you ready to begin an adventure that will challenge your thinking, improve how you communicate, and ultimately change your life? Join me as we bring forth the best "you" possible. Your life-changing journey begins the moment you turn this page.

Part I

Set Your Stage

- Strategy 1 -

KNOW YOURSELF

> **For I know the plans I have for you, declares the LORD, plans to prosper you and not to harm you, plans to give you hope and a future.**
> Jeremiah 29:11, New International Version

Find Your Purpose! We have choices to make in life. We can be effective or ineffective, powerful or weak, make a difference or settle for mediocrity. The choice is ours. Each individual must decide to simply exist or to live with purpose. It's unfortunate that some people choose to let life deal them a hand of complacency rather than to embrace God's best.

My mother passed away when I was twenty-two years old, I was really at a low. I didn't know what I was supposed to do with my life. My familiar world was yanked from under me. Nearly everyone around me had both parents and seemed very happy. I didn't know how to go on after losing the woman who had shaped my entire life from birth to young adulthood. I felt lost and for the first time in my life, I felt that I had no purpose or direction.

I voiced my feelings to a friend of my mother's, Dr. Pearl Singleton, the first lady of my church at the time. She immediately told me to pray and ask God to reveal my gifts and talents. I took her advice, and God responded. All of a sudden, I couldn't keep up with everything.

He truly showed me my worth, and then He set me on a path to create my world.

This tragedy in my life left me at a crossroad where I had a choice to make—to emotionally die or to live and get busy. I chose to live. My choice did not negate the incredible grief I felt in my heart because I missed my mother, but I could not allow the lies of the enemy to destroy my dreams and my purpose for being on this earth.

> **For some it takes lots of trial and error, and for others it's just logic, but you must find your purpose, a reason that you are here on this earth.**

For some it takes lots of trial and error, and for others it's just logic, but you must find your purpose, a reason that you are here on this earth. Tapping into it and actually fulfilling it is the challenge. If you have not yet chosen to live a purposeful life or if you don't know what it is, I encourage you to pray and ask your Creator to reveal your gifts and talents. The prayer can be as simple as this:

Father, help me to be all that You want me to be. Forgive my sins. You created me. I am asking You to reveal my gifts and talents and show me how I can use them while I am on this earth. I give You control of my life and ask You to build my world according to Your plan, not mine. Thank you, Lord! Amen.

My Purpose and Direction Is Communication!

God will bless you beyond your expectations with His response. For me, I know that my purpose and direction is communication. I have been given "the whole world of communication" and function in every realm of it. I've been blessed to teach and train individuals throughout the country. I have worked in the television/video industry for over thirty years and have worked in front of and behind the camera. My company specializes in TV/video productions, media consulting, public relations, and marketing. In addition to working with the broadcast and cable industries, I also write for print newspapers and magazines.

The emptiness I felt from my mother's death motivated me to pursue my purpose. However, the ironic part of this was that she had revealed it all to me before she passed away. I was chosen to be queen of an auto show in high school and became the representative for Chrysler. Along with that honor, I had the privilege to be interviewed by a local radio station. After my mother heard me speak, she told me, "You have a future in broadcasting." She was right, and today I am passionate about my work. The truth is, no matter what field anyone chooses, it all comes down to communication.

My life could have been completely different had I bought into a lie told in a senior honors English class. My instructor raised my paper up in front to the class and told them that I would never be a writer. I was devastated, embarrassed, and humiliated. From the way he talked, I was certain I'd received an F on that assignment, but he gave me a C. After that, when I wrote for print media, I included my maiden name in my byline, Bonnie Williams-Winfrey, so my instructor would see that I had become a writer. I humbly thank God for all He has allowed me to do in the field of media. At a recent class reunion, my instructor was there. I was respectful, but I told him how he humiliated me in front of my class and how the words he spoke over my life could have changed the course of how I pursued my purpose had I not believed in myself. He apologized and said he was glad I didn't listen to him.

Know that you were designed with a specific destiny and find out what it is. As you set your stage in life and begin to act upon it, don't internalize doubt and disbelief. Own your path!

Write the Vision

A simple stress-free life is a desire most would like to experience. Imagine being on an island alone or with people you enjoy, experiencing a beautiful oceanfront and listening as the waves bring harmony to create the best music you have ever heard. What a perfect, peaceful world!

Unfortunately, we don't live the perfect life. Challenges, difficult people, and our own insecurities share the stage in creating our world, whether good or bad, productive or unproductive. We live with difficult people, and sometimes we are those people. The way people communicate determines what type of person they are and who they attract to their world.

> **What's in the heart comes out in our communication and ultimately designs the road we travel.**

When it comes to writing the vision for our lives, we have choices. I think Michael Jackson's song, "Man in the Mirror" really drives this home:

I'm starting with the man in the mirror.

I'm asking him to change his ways,

And no message could have been any clearer.

If you wanna make the world a better place

Take a look at yourself, and then make a change.

Those humble lyrics challenge all of us to examine who we really are, and I encourage you to take this challenge as we take a close look at various types of difficult people we deal with in life. If we are going to write the vision for our lives, we will have to deal with what I call "road construction." As I describe such bumps, turns, and potholes that others cause in our day, we each must ask, "Do I act like that?" Such self-assessment is essential when dealing with difficult people because only through humility can we be part of the solution instead of being part of the problem. Let's start by looking at the heart. What's in the heart comes out in our communication and ultimately designs the road we travel.

What Does Your Heart Say?

The way to really know who a person is and what they are truly about is to look at their heart. Don't merely go by what they say because some people fight hard to stay where they are, and you need to weigh their actions against their words. Here are some examples.

Example1: There was an election in a particular city where the people had an opportunity to vote for progress and change. It was later reported that in one apartment building, there were three hundred registered voters. Their polling place was on the first floor of the building. A plea for residents to get out and vote rang across the community. After the election, it was learned that approximately twenty people from that building voted. This change could have brought better living conditions and a chance to live more independent and productive lives. What a tragedy! For some folks, it is easier to remain the same than to take a chance on change.

Example 2: Paul decided he was going to reward a group of people he felt was beneath him. The group and others thought this seemed to be a sincere gesture. However, upon further investigation, it was revealed that Paul was not using his own money to reward the group; he was using company funds. It was also learned that the day before Paul made this announcement, a co-worker was honored for helping people. When Paul saw the attention his co-worker received, he decided to do something similar, so he could be honored. The difference is, his co-worker was sincere and gave from his own resources; it was a kind gesture coming from his heart. However, Paul was motivated by recognition and missed an opportunity to show genuine love.

More Examples

Scenario1: Mary gave Jeff a card for Father's Day. Jeff was appreciative and said, "This card is really nice, and I think this card really describes me.

Mary then adds, "Yes, I always buy great cards."

Scenario 2: Judy wrote a very good article in the local newspaper about someone who was very deserving. Her husband, while at work, received multiple complimentary comments from his co-workers about his wife on her article, but each time he worked this statement into the conversation: "My wife thinks I am a really good singer." When he arrived home, he barely mentioned any of the compliments she received from his co-workers on her article.

Scenario 3: Bill explodes every time someone questions, criticizes, or points out a negative in his behavior. This out-of-control behavior is mostly seen among family members but rarely, if ever, by his professional acquaintances.

Scenario 4: Phyllis is very nasty to her husband behind closed doors. She deliberately keeps strife going in her home that not only affects her husband but also her children. But when the couple is in public or among friends she wants to impress, she puts on a grand performance, so anyone who sees them would think she really loves and cherishes her husband.

What is wrong in each of these four scenarios?

In Scenario 1, it's subtle, but Mary needed attention. As Jeff was enjoying the fact that he received a card he thought really reflected him, Mary inserts a cute comment to redirect the attention back to herself.

Jealousy is revealed in the second scenario. Judy's husband was jealous of his wife's spotlight moment. He couldn't just tell her all the nice compliments people gave her on her great article. Instead, he made a self-centered statement about himself to try to steal some of the attention his wife received.

Defensiveness, as displayed in Scenario 3, blocks growth. Bill has his guard up any time anyone says anything that remotely feels like criticism. As a result, he makes life miserable for those around him. They feel as if they are walking on egg shells. At some point, the victims in this case scenario may decide it is not worth the effort to communicate with Bill. In the end, if there is no change of behavior, Bill loses at connecting with people who love and care for him. People usually feel that he is not worth the fight they encounter when trying to give constructive criticism or offer viable suggestions.

Phyllis' behavior in Scenario 4 masks fear. She acts one way in public but another way behind closed doors. She's never real to others or to herself. No one really knows her because she's always playing a role. She doesn't know how to love or receive love because she fears the vulnerability of opening herself up to others.

While each of these four people displayed different behaviors, all of them are tied together by a common thread—insecurity.

What Is Insecurity?

Insecurity is described as a feeling of general unease or nervousness that may be triggered by perceiving oneself to be unloved, inadequate, or worthless (whether in a rational or irrational manner). A person who is insecure lacks confidence and questions their own value and capability. Seldom do they trust themselves or others, they have anxiety that a present, positive state is only temporary and will go wrong in the future and cause them loss or distress.

How Do You Know if You Are Insecure?

The best way to tell if you are insecure is by how you respond to the word *you*. When someone tries to talk to you and says things like, "You always," or "If you would only," does it hurt, bite, or scream at you? If you answered yes, then insecurity is a problem.

No one wants to admit they are insecure. We don't want to admit we lack confidence or struggle trusting ourselves and our decisions—but we all do at various levels. However, the red flag should go up when the word you rubs you the wrong way. It may be a sign and a symptom of a deeper issue, and if you do not face it and change your heart, it can ultimately destroy communication and relationships.

We don't want to admit we lack confidence or struggle trusting ourselves and our decisions— but we all do at various levels.

There is healing beyond the word you The answer is simple: change your heart, focus on others, and appreciate them by refusing to redirect the attention onto yourself. Put them in the spotlight and let them enjoy it! Allow others to love you and give you credit without trying to invent it for yourself. Last but not least, pray and ask God to help you. (See my prescription for overcoming insecurity in the Communication Clinic at the end of this book.)

Father God, You said "I am fearfully and wonderfully made." I need help in being all that You want me to be. Change the voices in my head that tell me I lack. Your Word tells me that anything I ask in Your name will be given according to Your riches in glory by Christ Jesus. I believe I am already secure and confident, becoming all that You want me to be. In Jesus' Name, Amen.

Create Your World

Communication is very crucial to our Creator. Just think, He literally spoke everything into existence. With His words—a command of His voice—He created our world. Note how God created through the spoken Word: "In the beginning God created the heaven and the earth" (Genesis 1:1, New King James Version).

It only took six days for Him to create it all and on the seventh day he rested. On day one, He simply said, "Let there be light' and there was light" (Genesis 1:3).

On day two, He said, "Let there be a firmament in the midst of the waters and let it divide the waters from the waters" (Genesis 1:6).

On day three, once again by a single command, He brought the waters under the heavens to be gathered together unto one place and dry land appeared (See Genesis 1:9). "Then God said, "Let the earth bring forth grass, the herb that yields seed, and the fruit tree that yields fruit according to its kind, whose seed is in itself, on the earth" (Genesis 1:11).

On day four, He spoke and made two lights, the sun and the moon, and He blessed us with stars (See Genesis 1:14).

Our whales and other creatures of the sea, as well as our feathered friends found their way into existence on day five at His command (See Genesis 1:20–21).

The beasts of the earth and man were created on day six. In Genesis 1:28, we read how God blessed Adam and Eve and told them, "Be fruitful and multiply; fill the earth and subdue it." "Then God saw everything that He had made, and indeed it was very good. So the evening and the morning were the sixth day" (Genesis 1:31).

What kind of world do we create with our words? Can we speak the words, "It is good!" and mean it? Our communication creates our world. I recently called a business office to inquire about some information I received in the mail. I greeted the woman by saying "Hi." I went on to tell her that I had received a bill and needed an explanation. With a mean tone and spirit she said, "What is the account number?"

I gave it to her, and I said nicely, "I think this is a mistake. I have great insurance and can't imagine that this amount was left unpaid."

She then hollered at me and said, "Just a minute; I am looking for it."

With respectful words and yet a firm tone, I told her that she didn't have to scream. She then hung up on me. I was left holding the phone wondering what happened. This woman was extremely rude. Her words were stiff and mean. Not only did I hear the unkind words oozing from this person, but I also felt her negative, cold spirit.

A day later, I again called this woman and was greeted with bitterness. I believe this negativity was coming straight from her heart. I was baffled by this lady, so I talked to someone else who had been in contact with her. They too were annoyed with her attitude. "As [a man] thinks in his heart, so is he" (Proverbs 23:7 am a, NKJV)).

Whatever we put out in the universe, we draw back to ourselves.

Again, what are we creating with our words? Whatever we put out in the universe, we draw back to ourselves. Proverbs 17:20 says, "He who has a deceitful heart finds no good, and he who has a perverse tongue falls into evil." I am not declaring negativity into this person's life; however, I am saying that she needs to change her attitude and speech to improve the quality of her life and the lives of those around her.

Declare and Decree

We are creators. We create what is spoken as God did when he created the world. Like God, our words also have power. In Job 22:28 (KJV) we read, "Thou shalt also decree a thing, and it shall be established unto thee: and the light shall shine upon thy ways." A decree is used to change a matter. It is spoken as a result of a decision. For example, I wanted to purchase an Italian vase my husband showed me in a store. I told him I could use it as a garbage can in a bathroom I was decorating. We noticed the only container in the store had a crack. I decided I still wanted it, but did not want to pay full price for it. I asked for a discount and was told by the cashier that nothing more would be taken off of it. It was already marked down to $20.00. I asked the cashier to get a manager. There was another girl standing nearby, and she offered to call a different manager than the one that was in the vicinity.

In the mean time, I was praying and asking God to give me my garbage can for $10. My words were: I declare and decree that this garbage can will be reduced to $10. Please give me favor with the manager. Speak to him and speak through me. The manager approached (very bubbly) and said, "Who requested me?" I responded and explained that I wanted the cracked Italian vase for a discounted price. He looked at me and inspected the item and said, "I am going to give it to you for $5.00." The original sales person was totally shocked with the discount.

I tell that story not because of a great deal I got on the vase, but because we need to know the power we possess simply by using our words. Words have power. When you decree something, you actually ask for it to manifest. What a powerful tool to make changes in our lives! We all have the power with our words to declare and decree that our communication is effective, our bodies are healed, and our dreams become reality.

Challenge

Discover your purpose in life by asking your Creator to reveal this knowledge to you. How can you create a more positive life and live it abundantly? Which of these principles are most helpful to more effectively use your communication skills to navigate through life's circumstances?

Declaration

I am purposefully living and fulfilling my destiny.

- Strategy 2 -

KNOW YOUR NEIGHBOR

> You shall not take vengeance, nor bear any grudge against the children of your people, but you shall love your neighbor as yourself.
> **Leviticus 19:18, KJV**

If communication was all about expressing our life's purpose to the world, it would be fun and easy. But it isn't. Like it or not, we all must communicate with not-so-lovely people along the way, and that makes life challenging and sometimes painful. That is why this communication strategy, Know Your Neighbor, is vital. We simply must learn how to communicate with many different types of people. The moral maxim "Do unto others as you would have them do unto you," also known as the Golden Rule, is a good standard when dealing with others and we need to use the same level of love and respect that we have received from our Creator. However, this command to love does not mean that you throw wisdom out the window. We are also commanded to be, "shrewd as serpents and harmless as doves" (Matthew 10:16).

With that being said, what happens when conflict arises? How do you handle it? You don't have to do one single thing to bring conflict into the communication flow. Some people thrive on it. Some people set you up for it, and others simply want to find out if you will crumble under the pressure. Many will try to wish it away. Some people get involved by going toe-to-toe with the person causing the conflict, while others ignore it completely, and yes, some fall apart. The proper way to handle conflict is to remain calm and try to resolve it.

There are negative people in this world. Negative or toxic people love to make others miserable. When dealing with this personality type, you must not show your weak side. Gain control of the conversation and don't take the irate person's comments personally. When you ecome involved with a toxic person, stay above the negativity and acknowledge it, but don't let it consume you. Let's look at some individuals with challenging behaviors, the difficulties those behaviors produce, and tips on how to handle them.

Meet the Faker

The faker has no real identity, and he's a control freak. He lives and speaks from a script he has written for himself. He's selfish and is all about bringing glory to himself, you cannot feel his heart. He plays a masterful game of having it all together to the public. When talking to him, the problem is never his and always yours. There is never any genuine ownership. He hides behind others to protect himself. He has the appearance of being bright but lacks intelligence. He has no real face or identity and lacks the desire to truly discover his own identity. In many cases, this person has experienced major rejection in his mind or in reality from a parent.

When you ecome involved with a toxic person, stay above the negativity and acknowledge it, but don't let it consume you.

The one thing you don't want to do with fakers is to take a seat on their roller coaster. If you do, it will be a ride to disaster. This type of communicator/personality type has only one agenda: self. Whatever it takes to control and demean, they will use it to preserve themselves.

Meet the Complainer

This person may look normal on the outside, but there is turmoil and negativity going on internally. For example, he can see that his wife has prepared a great dinner for him, but his appreciative words flow out as, "You left the light in the garage on all night. Why did you pull your car up so far in the garage? I am so sick of coming home and not being able to get in the door."

A few things are happening in this scenario: (1) His wife did not drive the car that particular evening; their daughter did. Thus the wife was falsely accused; (2) It was a mistake and not done to cause anxiety;(3) His wife was excited to share a nice evening, but her husband ruined the mood. She had worked diligently pouring love into the meal, and instead, his accusation threw a dark, damp cloud over the evening.

Phillip had a great idea to take his daughter out to the movies. She was thrilled. As they were preparing to get dressed for the outing, he said, "Hurry up! You're never on time for anything." (Note: Phillip was not dressed, either.) In a rough tone as he walks down the hallway, Phillip told his daughter, "Ruby, that outfit is too tight on you!" When Ruby gets downstairs, Phillip comments, "Hurry up and get your coat on; you always make us late!" (Note again, Phillip was not fully dressed.) When the two of them got into the car, he told Ruby, "I bet you didn't turn off the lights before you closed the door. You never do. I have to pay the bills, and you never think about that, do you?"

Before arriving at the movies, her father had already managed to verbally abuse her. She regretted accepting his invitation to be with him, and as a result she did not enjoy their outing.

Phillip observed that something was not the same and said, "What is wrong with you? Why are you so quiet?" She replied that she was fine. He proceeded to tell her, "I just took you to this great movie, and this is the thanks I get."

Once a complainer gets caught up in their own cycle of disengaging, it's hard for them to disconnect and find their way out of the maze they have created. They can destroy quality time with just a few words and complain about the littlest things, but they can never find fault with themselves. Like in the case with Ruby, she decided not to deal with the person, and she later filed her father away in the "people I don't like and don't enjoy being around" category. Ruby felt she could not be herself with her father, and no matter what she tried to do, it wasn't good enough for him.

Ralph got in bed and was enjoying one of his favorite television shows. He was laughing and relaxing after what he would call a challenging day. Mary walked into the room and observed him having a rare moment of excitement. She came to bed and said, "Why are you watching this when you know I have to get some sleep?"

He turns to her and says, "What are you talking about? You were downstairs watching what you wanted to watch before I came up." He goes back to watching his show.

She yells, "Would you please turn it down? You always have it up too loud. I want to go to sleep because I have to go to work in the morning. Remember, you can watch whatever you want, whenever you want while I am at work."

Ralph proceeds to tell Mary that he works just like she does and just because he is at home doing so, doesn't mean he is sitting around watching television. Ralph then turns the TV off because he became upset and lost interest in his program.

This was the wrong thing to do. Ralph let the complainer win. She can and most likely will come back even stronger. If Ralph turned off the television set to keep peace, that's one thing; but if Ralph gave in because he got mad, he just taught the complainer how to get her way. She becomes even more empowered. It's like a seed; once it is planted and watered, it continues to grow. The growth in this case is strife.

The conversation to have with complainers is to try to figure out the origin of their frustration. In most cases, they generally have a need and don't know how to communicate it. It is better to talk to them after they have calmed down. Once they get caught in their own world of misunderstanding, it is difficult to draw them out. Do not ignore the situation; if you do, it will come back to haunt you. Show them the good and possible positive outcome. All they can see with their negative glasses is the bad. One general rule of thumb to note here is that complainers usually target people they care about.

Meet the Alcoholic

Joyce appears poised to the public. There are no signs of alcohol on her breath. Her clothes are neat, and superficially she seems to be a likable person to those in her workplace. Ten hours later, she's verbally and/or physically abusive to her husband. Why, because he questioned her judgment on an issue, and she simply did not like it.

Communication with an alcoholic is difficult. They are usually good actors to those in authority, but they are transparent to family members and close friends.

The overuse of alcohol has a way of limiting intelligence as well as judgment. Their communication might be dummied down, their thoughts small, simple, and sometimes unrealistic. Control is usually an issue as the alcoholic is always trying to maintain it as well as demand it from others.

When communicating with an alcoholic, always remain in control, don't allow them to make you a victim; don't allow them to provoke you into becoming irate or irrational. Do not allow the alcoholic's lack of planning to become an emergency on your part. Speak slowly to the alcoholic, and remember, you aren't just dealing with a person inebriated and under the influence, but a negative spirit as well.

The best way to tame this personality type is to have an authority figure they respect involved in the communication. This is when you will see the alcoholic (for the moment) on their best behavior.

Nothing is ever good enough for this person. If you were to fix them a peanut butter and jelly sandwich, instead of them showing gratitude, they may complain about something as petty as the crust of the bread not being fresh. Say what you need to say and watch the theatrics begin.

I must caution you, when communicating with an alcoholic, always have a safety plan in place if you feel threatened and/or fear your life is in danger.

Meet the Identity-Problem Person

You may recognize this person by the term, "little man syndrome" or the "Napoleon complex." I recall a situation when Bob became very frustrated because a medical physician did not refer to him as a doctor. "How dare he not give title to me if he expects me to call him "Doctor"!

This man appeared to most people who knew him to be short, arrogant, and always bragging on his accomplishments. They described him as annoying at best. The conversation was always all about him, and he was never wrong. He worked all of his life to become big. He became a top political official. He took education to the highest level, hoping it would give him the status he was seeking. To make up for a lack in height, he often tried to make people feel beneath him. Even though he was seeking superiority to compensate for his height, he made himself look very small in the eyes of others.

The victim of "little man syndrome" is caught up in himself. He's never accepted who he really is and struggles to love the man God created him to be. It's hard for him to love others because of this deep-rooted dislike for himself. Unfortunately, this person rides through life fighting an internal battle that he's not aware of and never gets ahead emotionally because of his lack of awareness of this syndrome in which he is caught.

Watch the body language of this person. You will notice he is not really engaged with you. If he is sitting, his shoulders are pulled back away from you, at least one, if not both. You may be sharing in conversation, but this person is only after your respect which means acknowledging him as the center of the conversation. It is expected to use titles and refer to him as being important. This makes the "little man syndrome" victim feel safer. If his needs are not met, it is not uncommon to see and feel his rage. He is a master at using words to put people down.

The Napoleon complex was named after French Emperor Napoleon Bonaparte. Historians report that he compensated for his short stature by seeking power, war, and conquest. He lived his life thinking he was 5'2". Historians are now saying he was actually 5'6", and there was a mistake in converting French units of measure to English. The average height in the early 1800s was 5'5", so Napoleon wasn't really short. The illusion came into play because he was always with his imperial guards who were above average height and were considered tall.

The mind is powerful; it drives our body and tells it how to respond. Napoleon lived his whole life thinking he was short because of a measurement. He spent his time on earth trying to overcome a perception instead of valuing and loving the person he really was.

How do you communicate with this person? Very carefully; give him what he wants. Compliment him and then proceed with the rest of your business. It takes time in therapy to peel back all the layers of hurt and build this person to where he should be. Your purpose is for immediate action. There are many men short in stature, according to a measuring device, but tall because of who they are on the inside. If you are in a personal relationship with a "little man syndrome" victim, love the person and help him see his self-worth. It can be worth the battle when you win.

The Pretender

Words sputtered from this personality type are unpredictable. The person can come at you in one of two ways: normal and then loud or calm and then angry. If you disagree with them, they become extremely annoyed and upset. The interesting thing is you can actually see their rage heat up as if you are watching their imaginary thermometer. This person can be a hundred percent wrong, but they will still want you to validate them. If you disagree with them, you then become the person with whom they are angry. Communicating with a person with unpredictable rage is indeed a challenge. These individuals may suffer from alcoholic issues or mental problems. Everything in the person's mind may be interpreted as your fault.

People who overly indulge in drugs or alcohol are normally selfish. Their only concern is themselves. If they don't get their way, they may become angry, violent, and downright abusive. Exercise caution when you are in a heated battle with the spirit of negativity. This side can be extremely dark. Self-preservation is the key here. Do not internalize this person's pain. Remember, most people with personality disorders will try to control you, place demands on you, or name you as the problem if you go against their wishes. The pretender is no exception and has no problem disrespecting you. Do not allow this to happen. Address the issues with a firm voice and avoid becoming emotional. You hand over your power when you become emotional. This person then feels they can walk all over you.

Remember, most people with personality disorders will either try to control you, place demands on you, or name you as the problem if you go against their wishes.

Meet the Wannabe

Christy and George have been friends for thirty years. They work together and talk on the phone together just about every day. The two pretty much know everything about each other's lives, a friendship made in heaven. When the storms of life pounded their shorelines, they managed to stay afloat and comfort one another with support

The relationship flew in another direction when George was responsible for bringing a new employee into the company. Christy, immediately knew this person was bad news and did not have the best interest of the company at heart. The man proved to be selfish and mean-spirited, and because he could see that Christy saw that in him, he did everything in his power to remove her from her position by even attempting to destroy her reputation. Guess who helped him? Yes, George did. He sided with the manager to try and discredit Christy. The manager drew up false accusations about Christy and presented them to other staff. Her good friend, George, allowed it to happen.

George sacrificed his friendship with Christy for his own push for power. Wannabes have a desire to be accepted and respected, no matter what it takes. This person will lie and do whatever they can to place themselves in their desired position. Once in position, this person can also be territorial by protecting his or her environment. Webster describes the wannabe in this way, "A person who desires to be, or be like someone or something else." George's response to Christy was about having to do whatever it took to make the new boss successful. Christy asked him if he was willing to pay the price. Apparently he was, because he had a desire to climb to a higher level. However, the level desired in his head didn't really exist. George eventually fell from a healthy level of respect and integrity to one of disrespect. By the way, the boss eventually got rid of him and put someone else in his position.

To have a real conversation with a wannabe, keep them grounded and stick to the facts. Avoid entering into their world of boasting. Keep the topic of communication simple and focused to the issue at hand. Don't be fooled like Christy and always remember you are expendable.

Those Who Lack Confidence

One of the most challenging communicators to deal with (if you want accurate feedback) is one who has little or no confidence. The communication usually sways with the wind. This person seems to have little backbone. Why? Because they generally have shut down. He or she may actually try to take on your personality and be you. If you are a strong communicator, your personality and viewpoints could very well be mimicked by the person with self-esteem issues.

Signs of persons with negative image problems may be easily recognized. They avoid eye contact and a comfortable, firm handshake. Their body language, while standing or sitting, is not in an upright position. They tend to walk very slowly with their head slightly down. Confrontation is considered a sin and is avoided because their life is guided by fear and negativity. Silence is usually the preferred language.

This person works to protect themselves from aggressive personalities or those they think are wiser and superior. That's one side, but on the other side, this person may criticize you if you are speaking about them. Stop and listen. The same words you used to describe an action they committed may be reversed and thrown back in your face. This person may speak over you to keep from hearing what you are saying, but don't be fooled; they can hear what you're saying.

The person with low self-esteem may also beat themselves up when you say something less favorable to them. I caution you about using the word criticize because it doesn't have to be communication that is that strong. For instance, a simple statement like, "Your shoes don't match your outfit," can send them over the edge. It's all about how a person with poor image internalizes the world and what is being said about them. There is a voice inside the person with low self-esteem (which is actually a negative spirit) that constantly reminds them of their shortcomings, real or perceived. It screams words like loser and worthless into the recesses of their hearts. They hear, "No one will ever respect you because you never do anything right!"

When communicating to a person with low self-esteem or a poor self-image, it is crucial to compliment them. A simple comment such as, "That dress looks great on you," or, "That tie really goes well with your suit," will make a world of difference. Try everything you can to build them up. It can be difficult to obtain answers from this personality for two reasons: (1) They are reluctant to talk if they feel you aren't trustworthy, and (2) it takes energy on your part to communicate with them. We are put on this earth to value people and help them by looking past their faults. No one is perfect. The best way to deal with someone with low self-esteem is to help build them up and improve your relationship with them. Use body language as a tool. Move in closer to them, but don't invade their comfort zone. Make a connection by looking directly into their eyes as you speak. Most importantly, smile as much as you can to create a nonthreatening atmosphere. Use appropriate volume that is neither too loud nor too soft. If your voice is too intense, this person will shrink in body language. Watch your tone to be sure it is not too stern. Speak conversationally. People want to know they can speak with you and not feel threatened. In your conversation, allow a space for this person to respond and encourage their input. This lets them know they are important to the discussion.

We are put on this earth to value people and help them by looking past their faults.

Communicating with a Know-it-All

Know-it-alls want you to see communication one way only—from their point of view. No one knows everything. Intelligent people are usually smart because they listen to others, investigate what they don't know, and admit when they lack knowledge on a particular subject.

Know-it-alls have one focus, and that is to be the expert. They spend very little time listening and put a great deal of effort into controlling the conversation. Don't get me wrong; there is a distinct difference between an intelligent, wise person who is well versed and actually does know a lot about many subjects and the know-it-all who tends to be arrogant and insecure. When communicating, they tend to cut you off and nearly always steer you toward their opinion or solution, even though there may be several other potential solutions for said problem. They tend to be poor listeners because their thoughts and opinions are the only ones that matter. Know-it-alls are generally harmless, but they can be annoying.

The way to get your point across when talking to this type of communicator is to allow them to talk. Wait for the pause and then jump in with your opinion. Be prepared and have substance and facts to back up what you are saying. Body language is crucial here. Lean toward this person to let them know that they do not intimidate you. Look this person in the eye during the conversation and use your authoritative voice. This is not a time to be passive. Stay in control of your communication. When the know-it-all tries to cut you off, politely say, "Excuse me, I would like to finish making my point." This lets them know you are not a pushover. Watch the know-it-all's body language change to include you in the conversation.

The Selfie

In a phone conversation, Corine tells Bradley, her husband, that she may be late to a meeting. Bradley becomes frustrated and tells her that she is always late, and there is no reason why she should be. She tries to tell him what her challenges are, but he ignores her. He eventually tells her what he thinks of her and blames her for being late.

Corine was having problems getting to the meeting because she had to pick up one of their children from school later than usual. She then had to feed the children before going to the meeting. While traveling to the meeting, she found herself trapped in traffic beyond her control.

Bradley is considered by those who know him as selfish and a person who only thinks about himself. He only had one person to take care of—himself. Instead of offering words of comfort to Corine, he humiliated and demeaned her. She was taking care of her responsibilities as a mother.

Corine found herself in a no-win communication battle where she felt beaten. How do you communicate with a Bradley? Well, you don't. This person only looks at perspectives from his own selfish point of view. No matter what you tell him, in his mind, he interprets everything you say as excuses, and the selfish person victimizes himself. The targeted person has a choice to reject or accept accusations.

The best way to deal with this type of conversation is to end it. Yes, I rarely recommend hanging up on someone, but in this case, if you can't end the telephone conversation easily with the person who is putting you down, just hang up. First try words like, "Bradley, I tried to tell you what was going on. Do you want to hear my side of the story? I am not trying to be late. You have only one person to think about, and I have three others. If you can't listen to what I have to say, it is better for us not to talk right now. I will be at the meeting when I get there. I can't control the traffic flow." If the person doesn't comply, either say, "I'd rather not listen to what you are saying right now," or simply end the conversation.

This action allows the selfish person to reflect on his actions and hopefully calm down, call back, and apologize. When this happens, in Corine's case, it is important for her to tell her side of the story. Frustration builds, and this can be her way to free herself of some of the anger. No one wants to be demeaned, especially when they know they are doing something that needs to be done. The added stress is not necessary.

When confronting a selfish individual one-on-one, use your body language to create a disconnection with the person. By pushing one of your shoulders back, removing eye contact from the person, and focusing on something else, it shows this person that they are not the center of your universe. Wait for a pause in the conversation, lean forward with direct eye contact, and communicate your point by telling your side of the story. A selfish person must decide to respect and care about others. Telling a person, who only thinks of himself, of their need to change translates into your problem. How does one get around this attitude? Tell the person how their words affect you and how you feel. No one can argue with your feelings. In the case of Bradley and Corine, she could have said, "Bradley, when you talk to me in that tone, it sounds like I intentionally planned to be late. You really hurt me and made me feel worthless and unappreciated, and I am neither of those things."

> **When confronting a selfish individual one-on-one, use your body language to create a disconnection with the person.**

Another approach Corine could have taken was, "Bradley, you repeatedly put me down every time I do something that you don't like. This behavior is unacceptable. You are acting like a bully, and it seems like you only think of yourself. I'm tired of the way you are treating me." With this approach, Corine gives away her power. All Bradley can hear is one word—*you*—and he thinks even less of Corine. Then he intensifies the attack against her and the conversation then becomes a vicious losing battle until one person ends the conversation. Selfish and insecure people can't deal with the word *you*; it is like a sharp knife or dagger pointing at them and ripping them apart. In most instances, an abuser in their life used this word when hurting them. The word maneuvers throughout their spirit and burns.

The Repeater

Mary calls her sister, Mona, on a regular basis. Mona loves hearing from her sister. Mary starts a conversation with Mona, telling her she is fearful of going to the doctor because she doesn't want to find out if there is anything wrong with her. Mona tells her not to listen to fear and go to the doctor and find out if she is healthy. During their conversation, Mary continues to tell her story of fear to Mona at least three times. Mona is annoyed and can't get a word in.

Hector and Janey have been married nearly twenty years. Janey is excited when the two of them can find time to sit down and talk. She values the adult conversation and would like to get some things off her chest. In addition to being frustrated at work, she also has issues she'd like to discuss with Hector. An opportunity came when the two of them could talk. The children were gone, and the two of them were in the same room. Janey wanted to take advantage of this time.

While cooking dinner, Janey asked Hector to cut up a quarter of an onion for her. He started cutting the onion and said, "Is this how much you want?"

> Janey answered, "Hector, I asked you to cut up a quarter of the onion."
> Hector said, "Oh, you want a quarter of the onion cut?"
> Janey said, "Yes." She then asked him to cut up two stalks of celery.
> Hector asked, "Janey, are you sure you want two stalks of celery?"
> She snapped, "Yes."

Unfortunately, that is the way the night went with Hector repeating everything she asked of him and Janey's frustration intensifying. She confronted Hector about his repeating, and he said, "This is my new style of communicating." Needless to say, the important conversation Janey wanted to have with Hector never happened. As a matter of fact, he became irritated because she didn't want to play his little game.

It is common for people to repeat for clarity, understanding, and reinforcement. However, this is not what we are talking about in these two scenarios. In the situation with Mona, Mary carries on the whole conversation as if Mona is not on the other end of the telephone. Mona can and has in many cases put the phone down, walked away, and come back to find that she didn't miss one point in the conversation. Remember, Mary repeats whatever she is talking about several times. Mona finds herself repeating the same response. "Go to the doctor and find out if you are healthy...or not."

With Hector and Janey, Hector is playing a game and trying to get a rise out of Janey who doesn't want to play the game. She wants to talk seriously about something that is bothering her.

In both of these scenarios, the conversation literally stalled. Mary and Hector are both people who are touchy and will get offended if they feel they are being disrespected. The best way to handle repeaters is to remain calm and not gravitate. into the repeater's web, which only causes frustration. Point out that twenty minutes have passed, and it is annoying to be in a conversation that hasn't gone anywhere. Try to take control of the conversation to redirect it to another subject or to just end it on a positive note. Unfortunately with repeaters, there is little accomplished when communicating because they either talk over you or they communicate on an agenda of their own. This person is usually frustrated or disappointed when confronted. When you recognize you are involved with a repeater, the goal is to limit the conversation and redirect the conversation to a subject you both can mutually enjoy.

It's All about Them: Navigating the Pride Trap

Barry's life is all about Lights, Camera, Action! To the world, the life of Barry Johnson is polished and successful. He recently went on an exotic business trip, came back, and talked about his adventures and even bragged about the souvenirs he brought back to his children. To the outside world, he is admired for his work.

His wife tells another story. Barry went on his trip but didn't leave money or inquire if she needed money before he left. An incident occurred where he left his ties and wanted her to overnight them to him. This is when she found out he did not leave money in their account, which meant she could not get funds to send his ties or to meet her financial needs at home. From that point on, with four days left on the business trip, Barry never called her or the children to check on them. When he returned, he brought the four children and a couple of relatives gifts but didn't even get his wife a trinket. As a matter of fact, he got up the next morning without discussing anything with her and went out of town to visit a relative.

To the world, Barry looks like he had it all together. That was his goal. The only person who really knew his deceit, anger, and inability to commit to his immediate family was his wife. Barry is similar to many people who portray one image to the world and another one to their family.

Communication affects your present image, whether false or real, but it can also become a mirror that reflects your past. Barry's mother was an alcoholic. He never really had friends. But Barry and the rest of his family were very close. Why? Their bond was formed from the need to keep the secret of their mother's alcoholism and abuse. Still, that closeness was not healthy. In fact, Barry became so caught up with keeping his family's secret that he couldn't appreciate the blessing of having his own family and friends nor could he develop new and healthy relationships with others.

> **Communication affects your present image, whether false or real, but it can also become a mirror that reflects your past.**

Our past can impact our present communication. Barry developed a communication tactic of blame toward his wife and those who pointed out any little thing he did wrong. Every time his wife or others would confront him, he saw the image of his mother reflecting onto him. In his mind, he would never be like his mother, so he automatically rejected them and resorted to blame. Barry's wife was blamed for bad decisions he made with the finances, even though he controlled the money. She was blamed for him being mean to her. She was the reason for his out-of-control anger. Any time he didn't feel good about himself, she was the target of his fueled negative emotions.

So, how do you communicate with a person who is out of control and blames someone else for all their misfortunes? It is true - hurting people hurt people! In this case, it is very difficult because the person is very guarded, so stick to the subject! Don't get consumed in their world of anger and blame. Take control of the conversation and don't allow them to turn it back on you.

In this type of personality, he is his own cheerleader and tries to make others see how great he is. This type steers from any conversations involving true emotions - everything is superficial. When getting close to reality, the person may break down, turn on you, and become rude and defensive. You are now on the list with his wife. He's the victim, and you are to blame. This personality can't be criticized, and the word *you* rips them apart. This personality is very insecure, and *you* can't trust their behavior from one day to the next. The one thing to remember is you cannot make this person happy. If you know someone like this, it is important to completely understand that they are who and what they are, and it is not your fault. In life, we make choices; the best thing you can do is convince them to seek counseling and face the pain of their past.

This personality type works hard to cover up issues. In a relationship, there is always distance. On the outside, this person masks with nice clothes and a smile to play the part of having it together. On the inside, they are racked with fear in hopes that no one will find out who

they really are and see through their pretense. Their communication is about themselves and is very superficial. They are known to play an acceptance game of repeating something said in conversation or they ask an oh-so-obvious question to which everyone knows the answer.
The game continues their way as long as you allow them to play it that way. If you get off track and question anything, this personality immediately places you on their blame list at which time you can hear the rising defensiveness in their voice. You will also notice a lack of eye contact and/or see squirming in the person's body language. This personality type can be healed, if and only if, they want to be healed.

If you have to relate to this personality type, it is hard to win an argument. This person prides themselves on having the last word. Are you a Barry? Does the word *you* hurt when others try to confront you? In **Strategy 10: Let Your Body Speak**, you will learn about my prescription for handling insecurity.

Forgive and Forget

Relationships are built on give and take. It hurts when someone intentionally misuses trust. Have you ever been hurt by someone you thought would never betray you? Have you ever felt used? Have you ever had something stolen from you? If you have siblings, friends, or have done any work in corporate America, I'm sure the answer is yes. Brandi worked for a television station and felt she had a unique opportunity to educate the world about global warming and other atmospheric conditions. She thought since this specific station specialized in these matters, that it would be a great idea to become the authority. She went on a journey of clipping newspapers from all over the country as well as gathering other research and put together a proposal for management to consider. She submitted the idea to her boss, London, who then went to her boss. A show was developed and after producing the show and recruiting top experts to address the problems and render solutions, the ratings went up. The show was nominated for an award, and the station received notoriety through other media. However, she later learned that her boss, London, took all the credit for this new show.

Shortly afterward, Brandi learned that she would no longer produce the show. She was asked to continue to do research and gather guests, but she refused. She went back to her regular producing job. The ratings fell. Brandi was then asked to come back and produce the show again but refused. Because Brandi was the creator of the show and she was receiving a constant download of what would make the show successful from her Creator, her actions could not be duplicated. She eventually left the station.

Brandi was very disappointed and hurt following this incident. To move forward in healthy emotions, Brandi needed to forgive her boss. Without it, she would be giving her power over to London. God says, "Dearly beloved, avenge not yourselves, but [rather] give place unto wrath: for it is written, 'Vengeance [is] mine; I will repay'" (Romans. 12:19, KJV).This means that God will take care of this situation and any other hurts experienced.

We must forgive. How do you forgive when you don't want anything to do with the individual(s) who hurt you? You just do it! Choose to forgive because God commands us to forgive the person(s) seventy times seven. It's not always easy depending on the situation. Surrender the problem to God. Forgiveness is not for the other person. It is for your benefit and peace of mind. When we are clogged up with hate, anger, resentment, pain, strife, and rage, we are only hurting ourselves. It hurts our health, our mental well-being, and our other abilities. Joselyn was hurt by her sister who did some awful things to her. Joselyn was told by another friend she had a problem with forgiveness. Joselyn held a grudge and would not speak with her sister for months. If the sister was in her presence, she didn't see or acknowledge her and considered her dead.

Unforgiveness works like a sword piercing your heart and slicing pieces from your soul. Many times we feel frustration toward the person who harmed us, but the real intent of unforgiveness is to destroy you. It's like a disease that eats away at your core. People often say, "I forgive him or her, but I surely won't forget what he or she did to me." True forgiveness means you hand over to God that person and the hurt they caused you. It goes further; God tells us in Luke 6:27–28 to speak a blessing over those who curse us. This act frees us, and God will take care of wrongdoers because He has a love for justice and will restore and repay us for everything that has been taken from us.

The reason unforgiveness/forgiveness is mentioned in this section of the book is because the lack of forgiveness is sometimes the key to prohibiting us from being all we should be and building healthy and positive relationships. Medical studies have concluded that over sixty percent of all chronic illnesses are rooted in anger and unforgiveness. Being part of this statistic is not healthy, and it certainly does not bring about longevity or happiness.

Stay Calm and Move On: Letting Go of Past Hurts

Alex was in the army for four years. Prior to volunteering for his country, he was a lively, energetic person. Seeing his fellow service companions gunned down during the Korean War changed him. He also was shot in the line of duty. After the incident, his personality was quieter. His excitement for life diminished, and he seemed to shut down. His mental, physical, and emotional battle scars affected his communication.

Tom, a white man, learned that his great-grandfather was killed by an Asian. No one really knew the true story. Rumor had it that his great-grandfather was threatening a young Asian man and in self-defense, the man murdered him. Tom's hurt led him to dislike every Asian he encountered.

Mildred was raped at the age of fifteen. She was minding her own business walking down a street when two men pulled her into an alley, jumped her, and brutally assaulted her. Mildred is now fifty-two, and this violation continues to hold her in a fear mode. She refuses to go anywhere by herself. She doubts herself, and she doesn't trust any man.

In all three of these situations, past hurts have altered lives and changed the way they communicate. Pain in the past can control one's present.

Pain can teach and mature us, but it is never to stifle us. It is crucial to become free from the bondage that holds us hostage.

Past hurts can transition us from one state in life to another. Proverbs 4:23, Amplified Bible says, "Watch over your heart with all diligence, for from it flow the springs of life." Unresolved past hurts can drive a person to drink, use drugs, or isolate—whatever it takes to anesthetize the pain. Imagine living in a bubble where negative talk invades every thought. When you think you have done something well, the devil tells you it wasn't good at all. When someone tells the victim of past hurts that they are a great and funny person, they filter that comment in their mind, place it into the "not true" bucket, and replace the compliment with a lie, which translates to something like, I'm an awful, horrible person that nobody loves.

Here is a simple way to forgive and be free by using visualization and the power of words.

Take each member of your family and the people who have hurt you and imagine them in front of you, one at a time. Look them in the eyes with sincere love coming from your heart, then say these words that my friend, Karol Truman, author of the book, Feelings Buried Alive Never Die, shared with me:

"I behold you with eyes of love and glory in your perfection. If I have ever done anything that has hurt you or caused you pain or sorrow in any way, will you forgive me? I am truly sorry." Wait a few seconds then say, "Thank you, (person's name), I love you!"

Then see yourself giving them a loving hug and feel and accept the change that comes from going through this process.

Challenge

Identify behavior(s) in your personality that are similar to those mentioned here. Which is the most difficult for you to accept about yourself? What steps are you willing to take to change the way you communicate? Who do you need to forgive in your life? What is preventing you from taking action?

Declaration

I am whole—mentally, physically, spiritually, and emotionally.

- Strategy 3 -

IDENTIFY YOUR ENEMY

> Be sober, be vigilant; because your adversary
> the devil, as a roaring lion, walkers about,
> seeking whom he may devour.
>
> **1 Peter 5:8, KJV**

Most behaviors mentioned in the last strategy, although irritating and frustrating, are tame compared to those we will look at now. We have discussed people who are identity confused, insensitive, or uncaring, and while they really don't mean to harm anyone, they have little to no clue of how their behavior affects those around them. However, there are those with an agenda, and they are downright dangerous. They have wounded spirits and truly enjoy hurting others. It is important to distinguish between the two for your own safety and mental health because communicating with them—especially in a family or work situation—can be very painful and/or costly. While our politically correct society pretends that there are no real enemies, I say there most certainly are, and we would be wise to identify them so we can protect ourselves while communicating.

The Narcissist

One of the most agonizing personalities of them all is the narcissist. This personality type is the center of their universe. They are controlling and demand for you to fall in line. Often they'll deny their mistakes and quickly point out how you are at fault. They generally do not like themselves and crave praise from others.

I remember sitting in church and listening to an associate minister excessively praise his wife before every sermon. It was so predictable that the congregation grew to expect it. She was a true narcissist, and he was great at meeting her needs. You could notice a big difference in her posture and actually see her face light up.

Control

The narcissist has to have control over all situations. Kelly can't even go out to dinner with her friends and enjoy a simple evening. She's the one bossing the staff, setting up the seating arrangements, and in some cases running the entire evening. Her friends don't like it, but they accept her behavior and chalk it up to her way. If confronted, she often becomes angry. Kelly craved praise so much that one of her goals in life was to do something special and big, not for the joy of helping people, but for the recognition.

Narcissists normally surround themselves with people who keep them on the throne of their universe. They have to feel safe and know they have the loyalty and praise of those around them.

Narcissists normally surround themselves with people who keep them on the throne of their universe.

Rudy is the newest president positioned into a corporation after the former CEO retired. When people say "no" to him or disagree with him, he gets rid of them. He ultimately developed his own little universe of "praisers"—his leadership team—whom he could easily control and manipulate.

The difference between a narcissist and a well-adjusted person is that narcissists only look out for themselves and for what is important to them. The well-adjusted person thinks about others and pulls people together to bring forth the best solutions. The focus is not just on themselves, but all involved.

Fear

You may have heard the definition of fear as False Evidence Appearing Real, but what is fear to the narcissist? Many of them rule by fear with the expectation that people should feel threatened by them. How does this happen? If you do not fall in line and function comfortably with the rules set by the narcissist, you immediately become a target for termination or dismissal. Internally, the narcissist's greatest fear is that they will be found out (even though they may or may not know who they really are), so their only goal is to keep control over you, to keep you feeling uneasy. They feel they are God. They rule and you must obey or be slaughtered. Followers are subservient and are treated as less intelligent.

A young minister approached his seminary instructor and told him he didn't agree with his interpretation of the Bible on a matter he spoke about in class. The teacher proceeded to tell him that he didn't get it because his perception was off and then proceeded to persuade the young minister that he was the problem. Disconcerted, the young minister went to his pastor and, without mentioning what his instructor said, asked him to interpret the Bible passage discussed in class. His pastor had the same interpretation as the young minister and scripturally proved it as well. Upon receiving this second opinion, the young minister realized his instructor's lack of knowledge but was completely stunned when his instructor immediately ostracized him and did not allow him the special privileges granted to other students.

A successful business woman had been working with a company as a vendor for a number of years, giving them exceptional exposure.

When the company hired a new leader, he demanded the business woman give him her client list. He told her that he was going to call her clients and ask what they were paying for her services. The new leader had not asked this of any other vendor, and he was well aware of the success she had brought to his company.

The business woman politely refused and explained that she was protecting the confidential rights of her clients; however, she was willing to provide him with references, even though she had been performing the service for a number of years. He then told her he would be replacing her as a vendor. To show good faith, she provided him with a number of materials to show the worth to his company. He later tried to paint her as a thief because she rejected him and his request.

In both of these incidents, fear was the driving force. In the narcissist's universe, fear is always present. They fear life, they fear their own fears, they fear losing control, and they fear any threat or perceived threat to their self-esteem or worth. They are never wrong, and they feel no need to change. When their ego is threatened or when they are not the center of attention, they strike, typically in a mad rage.

In the example of the young minister, what was the fear factor? The narcissist in this case could not be wrong and shouldn't be challenged. The respectful, mild, and meek young man, in the eyes of the narcissist, was supposed to be less knowledgeable than the instructor. How dare he confront and challenge the narcissistic teacher! You have to understand that in the narcissist's mind, superiority reigns supreme. This type of personality avoids criticism, confrontation, opposition, and competition. Anything perceived to pull down self-worth is avoided.

The example involving the business woman soured when she declined to share documents with the new executive. The conversation became explosive. It's not uncommon for the narcissist to become enraged, damage property, hurt people, lie, or become verbally abusive. In the narcissist's mind, they are always the victim. This personality will do whatever it takes to restore the ego, no matter what the cost—even if it means devaluing others to gain superiority.

Narcissists usually pursue top positions. When in place, they feel empowered and accomplished, particularly when stripping others they deem as a threat of power. Unfortunately, the narcissist still suffers pain. They always worry about how they are perceived by people, how to perform at certain events, and how to look and be in charge in different scenarios. The threat of being offended is always there. Their own ghosts constantly haunt them. The thought of feeling like someone would think of them as unworthy or inadequate is a fight the narcissist constantly lives with.

Enemy

In a normal person's life, there is a desire to love and be loved. To be emotionally connected is a good thing but not to the narcissistic personality type. The narcissist craves praise; this is love to them.

The quest for real love is how the term narcissus was born. In Greek mythology, a character who was so in love with himself saw his reflection in a pool of water. He became so enchanted with his own reflection that he eventually fell into the pool and drowned. It was believed that he came back to life in the form of a flower (hubris) that blooms once a year. The moral of the story is that narcissists eventually drown in their own world of false illusions without knowing who they really are.

The narcissist views people having a different opinion as threatening. Those with opposing views are often considered an enemy. A relationship has very little meaning to the narcissist and generally represents the means to an end.

Kate found herself in a disturbing conversation with her male boss. She tried to discuss strategy about a particular issue. Her boss told her he didn't care about the past or any other background information she was trying to supply. He stated, "All I want is what I want done." She was stunned. The boss was new to the job, and she was just trying to show how and why a certain protocol was put in place.

Identifying Character Traits of a Narcissist
- Does the person lack empathy?
- If you are working on a project together, are you doing the bulk of the work when you are supposed to be sharing duties?
- Does the person lack original ideas and mirrors others' ideas?
- Does the person become irate if the topic of discussion is not about him or her?
- Do you feel highly stressed around this person?
- Does this person delegate work (which is his/her responsibility) and then micro-manage everything?
- Does this person cheat?
- Does this person take care of his or her own needs and desires before that of the organization or business?
- Does the person speak for the organization or business from an inclusive "I" or "my staff" perspective, speaking for everyone else without even consulting them?
- Does this person accept praise for good results but blames others for negative results?

If you answered "yes" to most or all of these questions, the person is probably a narcissist. The best test of all is for you to determine if you can feel the person's heart or not. Does this person genuinely care for those in need or others in general? Look for actions, not words. When you see a gesture of kindness, make sure there is no benefit to the narcissist.

The Script

The narcissist's conversation usually flows from a script he or she has memorized. I remember talking to a group of people in a hallway, and a known narcissistic person saw me and then aggressively flew around the corner and later came back and said, "Hi, Mrs. Winfrey how are you?" I thought the behavior was unusual, but it became quite evident after repeated acts on different occasions that the person saw me unexpectedly and didn't have his script prepared. After he went around the corner, he gathered his lines and was able to approach me. When the narcissist's script is edited by whoever they are talking to, that is when you are more likely to catch them off guard. Many times a reaction is a laugh, but note, the person may be laughing at you. The reaction may even be one of rage, where the person either runs away from the situation or tries to reinforce their authority over you.

> **The narcissist's conversation usually flows from a script they have memorized.**

What the narcissist is really trying to do is show you who is superior. This is the time to trust your instincts. Examine how you feel while talking to the narcissist. That feeling is usually negative. He can become extremely negative and/or violent as mentioned earlier if you say the word *no*. That is the word that can send the narcissist into the red zone.

Communicating with a Narcissist

Even though the narcissist thinks the person who wounded them is the enemy, their real enemy is within. The big question is how do you communicate with a narcissist? Well, you must have your i's dotted and t's crossed at all times. They view this as a war game, and it is usually their time to attack. Never forget that you are the enemy. This is the time to feed the beast by knocking him off his game with compliments. The "feed the beast" term is often used in corporate America. If you feed the beast, it becomes manageable and friendly, and you can pet it without being bitten. If you don't feed the beast, you could become its food of choice. Please note that when the narcissist feels threatened and inadequate, they will choose someone else to do their dirty work. This person is generally a "praiser," someone who has their back and will help the narcissist remain superior and in control.

What do you do when you are set up? Just stick to the facts and evidence and try to have witnesses to back your side of the story. The narcissist is good at creating a fight and making the opponent the one to prove innocence. Remember, this person is never wrong. Don't allow yourself to become boxed into this web of destruction. Rise above it by staying focused on the truth. Your attitude should be one of looking at the big picture and talking about how the situation or argument will benefit the subject discussed.

Warning: Do not stay on the same level as the narcissist. They play the game better than you ever will. Get out of the web to maintain your own sanity. Remember you have power, and that is why they consider your presence to be a threat.

It can be very exhausting dealing with this personality type. The question is this: Why doesn't this person spend their time doing something more constructive? Even though the narcissist claims the victim role, the true victim can really be the person with whom they are speaking.

Agatha remembers talking to a person who would not give into her, and Agatha actually hit the other person and then falsified facts to investigating officials, saying she did not do it. Another person in the room with Agatha witnessed the incident and also lied, stating there was no assault. The witness was her "praiser." It's interesting how this type of loyalty works.

Gordon recalls the time when he was in a situation where he told the narcissist that he would surrender and do whatever she wanted. He knew she would fail if he withheld details that she did not know. The narcissist became frustrated. Gordon gave up his control and surrendered to her request. However, she felt and knew he was still in control, even though he gave into her demands. This behavior sparked even more negativity and rage. It did not end well for either of them.

The Liar

"Hurt" is the reaction most people feel when someone purposefully lies with specific and deliberate intent It was Milton's wedding day. He was so excited about marrying the woman of his dreams. It was the wedding of the century: ten bridesmaids, ten groomsmen, and all the trimmings of a royal wedding were all part of the fanfare. What he didn't know was his bride had a secret. Several of his groomsmen knew about it. His bride had a secret life and was previously married and had two children being raised by her ex-husband. After the couple's honeymoon, one of the groomsmen felt guilty about keeping the secret and told Milton the truth. Milton was hurt, disappointed beyond words, and felt he was intentionally deceived. He confronted his wife; she apologized and vowed to make up for the deception. After two years, the marriage ended because the trust was broken. It just went out the window. Milton felt the marriage was not built on a foundation of trust, and if she could lie about that, he couldn't help but wonder what else would be revealed later in life.

When communicating with a liar, listen to your instincts. If you have a discerning spirit, you will know the difference. Lies speak to us. The person's eye contact is usually not engaged. The person may look away but will very seldom look you in the eye. The body posturing of the person almost always shifts to a nervous, fidgety, or closed positioning. Hands may be stern and gripped to a crossed or locked position either in front or behind the body or the hand is placed inside pockets of clothing. Lies may also force the person telling the lie to move with nervous energy. Then, there are others who are so good at lying that they rarely show any signs.

For the most part, we trust people and want to take people at their word. But if something doesn't feel or sound right, or if the body language contradicts what the person is saying, these are usually signs that someone is telling an untruth.

Why do people lie? Everyone has told a lie in some point of their life. We are not perfect beings. Some people lie excessively because they want to be portrayed or perceived as someone they are not. Some want to hide something they have done or said. Some feel it is the ultimate way to make something disappear. If you lie about it, it doesn't exist. Others have talked themselves into a different definition of the word and actually believe what they are saying.

June grew up in a family that told her that she and her sisters and brothers were better than everyone else. Unfortunately, this "brainwashing" birthed an elite attitude among the children. These children were told a lie; they believed it and lived it. When the real world hit them, and they had to survive outside of the cocoon that poisoned them, they were shocked that the world did not revolve around them nor did it perceive them as better. The imaginary world they lived in was nothing more than a lie. The lie prohibited both parents and children from being all they could be and living to their fullest potential.

Communicating with a liar can be very difficult. Do not internalize their problem. Do not own the mess they've created. Depending on your personality type, some people may try and turn the tables and tell you that you caused them to lie. The blame is now placed on you. If the person with whom you are talking is a really good liar, you can be sent on an emotional wild goose chase. In some cases, you become the liar in their eyes, and the act in question is something you committed or caused. Again, stay focused on the issue at hand. Communicate only to the action. If a person continues to try to lie their way out of the situation, stick to the facts, lay down whatever consequences are relevant, and speak from the standpoint of the evidence you have obtained.

Some folks live by the lie, and their whole existence revolves around it, like in the example of the children who were taught they were better than everyone else. People want to be seen as good in the eyes of others. If lying will get them there, it becomes their weapon of choice in protecting their image.

The Deceiver

Trust is a big part of open communication. When two people are communicating and trust is among them, understanding can be a result of the communication. A relationship can be strengthened, and results can be obtained. Jessica and Joann have been good friends since college. Jessica knows that Joann has her back, and she can confide her deepest secrets and worst fears to Joann and know that she will not be judged or criticized because of her shortcomings. The two of them share things they feel will stay between them. That's trust.

When trust is not in the communication, there can be a discord where talks are shortened, falsified, or completely cut off. People want to feel that they can trust the person with whom they are speaking. We have a natural instinct to protect ourselves from those who wish to bring harm to us, whether it's perceived or real fear.

Joe and Fred were members of the same football team. Both watched for that special gleam in the scouts' eyes that would spell out college scholarships for them both. Fred told Joe that he got a call from the University of Illinois. Joe said, "They are looking at me, too!" One day Fred answered a call from the coach who advised him that he had received an anonymous phone call from one of his teammates. Fred's peer spoke negative words about his relationship with other teammates and said, "He is hard to get along with, and he falsified his ability and performance." Fred knew immediately who the person was. He had only told one person that the university was possibly going to offer him a scholarship.

When you trust someone and find out that this trust has been violated, how do you communicate? The answer is, with caution. When it is known that someone does not have your best interest at heart, tread lightly. First of all, don't assume you are a hundred percent right with your assumption. There is a chance you could be wrong. Remain calm, acknowledge the situation, and if you feel led to confront the person, do not allow them to stir you to anger. When someone isn't in your corner, they can turn the facts and make up issues about you. For instance, "Fred, I have been your friend for over six years. How could you possibly think I would do something like this to you? I thought you and I were best friends, and you trusted me."

Don't get caught in the web of the guilty party. Emotion is brought into play, and your loyalty is questioned. The way to avoid this maze is to stick to the fact. "Joe, I am having a problem with this because I only told one person about the school looking at me. When I look at the facts, I wonder how anyone else would even know about this, so I am asking you. I would hope you wouldn't talk against me when you know how important this scholarship opportunity is for me, not to mention the opportunity to play with such a great team."

Fred remains in the driver's seat of this conversation and gets his point across. He keeps his dignity and integrity in check while Joe's tactics to make him feel guilty fizzles.

Handling the Enemy

Choose to be an eagle. Do not squander your time or talent with the chickens. Try to keep respect on both sides of the table and definitely demand fairness and respect for yourself. Do not be overthrown with character assassination attempts, arrogant displays, bully attacks, or lack of empathy. Soar above the situation. Keep your body language upright (no slouching) and your eye contact direct. "When a man's ways please the Lord, He makes even his enemies be at peace with him" (Proverbs 16:7).

Own character. Dr. Oby Ezekwesili, co-founder of Transparency International, says she learned the following wisdom from her father. "You don't have character until you have consistent character."

Challenge

Choose not to be an enemy. If you find that you reflect any of the personality traits mentioned in this strategy, choose to be better. Which techniques do you see yourself using as you deal with your enemies?

Declaration

I am protected from my enemies. I have a shield of protection in me, on me, and through me. I have consistent character. I manage my emotions and my response to others. I use my power to set my stage positively.

Part II

Own Your Stage

- Strategy 4 -

PREPARE YOURSELF

> **Do your planning and prepare your fields before building your house.**
> Proverbs 24:27 New Living Translation

What do Michael Jordan, Tiger Woods, LeBron James, Gale Sayers, Arthur Ashe, Stephen Curry, Babe Ruth, Muhammed Ali, Joe DiMaggio, Jerry West, Walter Payton, and Venus and Serena Williams have in common? They are all known as some of the greatest athletes of our time. Besides greatness, they also share a common bond. This single quality helped to launch them into the history books. It is called "the prep." They have all practiced and perfected their crafts. They have put in countless hours in developing their bodies and strategies that have helped them become Hall of Famers and/or national sports icons.

The strategies are no different for you and me when it comes to communicating. We must have a game plan to develop our communication success, and it is called "the prep."

To command your world and be an effective communicator, one must prepare for the job. We've all heard the saying, "A man without a plan plans to fail." In order to own your own stage, it is vital for one to physically, mentally, and spiritually be prepared for the task ahead.

Case Study: Ginger Miller

Ginger Miller is expected to address her corporate bosses with a plan to integrate technology that will boost productivity for the company.

Ginger's immediate boss chose her for the presentation because of her technical expertise. She is known at her branch as a technical genius. Ralph, Ginger's boss, has full confidence that she will represent well and sell the executive team on the concepts she has designed that will ultimately save the company millions of dollars.

There is one problem. Ginger does not share her boss's belief, and she does not like public speaking. She actually hates it. She doesn't really like being around people. She feels paranoid when she is in front of a group, and she feels the people around her dislike her. Ginger is good at designing concepts but presenting them is her worst nightmare. Ginger only has one month to get ready for her presentation.

It is key to make sure one's physical self does not break down on game day. Improving overall health in the physical realm is not only important in everyday living, but in public speaking as well.

My former fitness coach often told me, "Exercise is the key to the fountain of youth." He's made a believer out of me. He's been a bodybuilder for years and has won many national competitions, and you would never know this man is in his late fifties. When you see the people he trains, they all look young as well.

Looking good and feeling good are all attributes we want to have when presenting. In my communication clinics, I advise all my clients to exercise at least three days a week. I personally work out five days a week because I am one of those people who enjoys exercising.

Ginger has agreed to a regimen of three days a week. I hope within two weeks, she will increase her workout to four days. Ginger is not fond of exercising and has not really participated in an organized fitness plan since high school, which was twenty years ago. She carries an extra twenty-five pounds and doesn't like to move around. I recommended she walk at least thirty minutes three days a week for the first two weeks. This has been a chore for Ginger because she works long hours and says she doesn't have any time to herself. I have instructed her to take this walk during her lunch hour, and it seems to work. What she doesn't know is that exercise builds endurance, and by improving her health physically, she will also improve her ability to speak.

Step one for Ginger is physical exercise. Step two is integrating inhaling/exhaling breathing techniques to help her with breath control. When people are not used to delivering presentations, it is very common for them to run out of air. In addressing Ginger's presentation skills, I found that one reason she struggles when speaking is her smoking. The immediate answer would be to quit smoking. But when a person is nervous because of a task they really prefer not to do, it is better to work with them until they can quit on their own.

To prevent and combat breath control issues, I prescribed techniques for Ginger to work on.

1. Exercise breath control. Breathing into full lung capacity for ten seconds, holding for five, and slowly exhaling (pucker lips) for ten helps in exercising for better breath control. This technique expands lung capacity and should be performed at least ten times a day. Once it is mastered, it should become a daily routine for life.

2. Read long sentences. The goal here is to not hold in air and gasp for breath in the end. An example would be:

> *The Library of Congress is offering a once in a lifetime opportunity for anyone who wants to have their books, music recordings, video productions, and any other original, written copy to go to their local public libraries between the hours of 9 a.m. and 5 p.m., and they can do so in half the time it normally takes.*

This extended sentence could send one running out of breath easily. The goal for Ginger is to be in control of this sentence and make it work for her. In order to do this, it is important to place commas in places to remind her to breathe. She will take advantage of some that are present and create her own to help the sentence flow within her ability. After running out of breath five times, we redesigned the sentence to read:

> *The Library of Congress is offering—a once in a lifetime opportunity for anyone who wants to have their books, music recordings, video productions, and any other original, written copy—to go to their local public libraries—between the hours of 9 a.m. and 5 p.m. and they can do so—in half the time—it normally takes.*

Of course, my normal instinct would be to rewrite the sentence completely, but the purpose of this exercise is breath control. The sentence is designed to be extreme. Ginger has done a great job making it work for her. Her dashes indicate additional breathing. This exercise lets her know she has control over her breathing.

We now move into the area that Ginger dislikes the most: a voice checkup. From the time she was a little girl, she has been criticized for having a soft, somewhat squeaky voice. She says she cringes every time she listens to a personal recording. That's because what Ginger normally hears is her voice through her inner ears, not what the world hears with outer ears. She is more familiar with this voice than the voice an audience would hear. The goal is to improve and like both voices.

Confidence

It is not uncommon for people who fear communication to choose fields such as technical ones to avoid face-to-face communication. The reality is everyone will have to communicate. In Ginger's case, she never expected it to be taken to the level of presenting to executives.

There is one word that is a secret weapon when it comes to communicating. It is confidence. When it is there, you can see it, feel it, and even desire it. When it's not there, it boggles the human mind. It's like baking a cake without the sugar when the recipe calls for it.

If confidence is not detected in the voice, it can alter results. In the case of Ginger, her message and her power of persuasion should be one that will hopefully change the focus of her company. Her voice can't be wimpy.

There is good news about correcting voice issues, and there is a happy medium. After a series of testing through scripted reads and general conversation with staff, I determined that Ginger's rate of speaking is slow; her vocal tone is friendly, which is good, but her vocal volume is way too soft. The spectrum for the rate of speaking is from fast to slow. I think we can all identify with people who speak way too fast, and you can't get a word into the conversation. Then again, there is that p-e-r-s-o-n w-h-o d-r-a-g-s o-u-t t-h-e c-o-n-v-e-r-s-a-t-i-o-n.

As far as vocal tone, we can generally feel it. It is easy to detect if someone is being friendly or if they are on the other side of the range that falls into the boisterous category. Then, there are those who speak with a volume that is either too soft or too loud. The goal is to tailor your rate of speaking to a medium range (not too fast or too slow), and use a vocal tone that reflects friendliness in the conversation. Vary the vocal volume for emphasis but keep it in between the wimpy voice and the boisterous voice. Some people think you can't talk about a serious subject without being stern. This is not true. You can be serious about an issue but still be friendly and conversational. To reach a level of confidence, you must at least have these essential ingredients:

Friendly + conversational + flexible appropriate vocal volume = confidence

To adjust Ginger's voice, we determined she needed an overhaul. Sometimes pain from one's past can alter one's star quality in communicating. In the clinic, she's learning how to integrate deep tones into her speech. To try this, take a deep breath(breathe in for ten seconds, hold for five, and out again for ten) and speak as you let out the air. The speech comes from the diaphragm. You can clearly hear the deep tones. Ginger was guilty of talking from her throat. This new quality added more substance to her voice. I sped up her rate of speaking by integrating fast phrases into her speech pattern. She normally sounded like a broken record with the same drawn-out, slow rate. To give you an example, this sentence was previously read as, "The appropriate approach to finding the results would be to allow everyone to take the survey." Ginger now reads this as, "The appropriate approach (from a medium speed to a slightly faster speed) to finding the results would be (medium speed) to allow everyone to take the survey" (not raising her voice as a question on the last word).

Elevating the volume in Ginger's voice is a challenge. Hidden insecurities sometimes manifest within the voice, causing one's self-esteem to beat down vocal volume. I am not saying that all people with soft voices are insecure or have low self-esteem. I am saying, however, a great number of men and women who lack confidence or have low self-esteem do speak with low volume. On the other hand, many men and women who speak loud or with boisterous tones can also be guilty of low self-esteem. The loud voice is usually the mask. In one of my sessions, one administrator told me that he purposely speaks in a loud manner because it is threatening. He shared with me that he was taught this technique in college.

Well, unfortunately, the joke is on him. People who live to threaten are folks no one really wants to be around. Their insecurities are usually exposed as people spend more time with them.

The right response for Ginger and all of us is to keep the voice interesting and talk with a medium volume that everyone can hear. For emphasis and when appropriate, volume can be adjusted and integrated to make a point. Ginger needs to travel out of her comfort zone. When raising her voice one octave, she feels she is yelling. Again, she doesn't hear what her audience hears. Her voice seems louder to her. To get Ginger beyond this point, the answer is not necessarily for her to speak louder but to work on ways for her to love herself and her voice.

For emphasis and when appropriate, volume can be adjusted and integrated to make a point.

•**Step 1:** Ginger must love herself. The plan to get her there is to change her perception from the inside out. Life hits us all. What do we do with the pain we suffer? Ginger was molested as a child. She swallowed her emotions and tucked this pain away, but those feelings don't stay buried. I have recommended this affirmation for her: "I am beautiful. I am a great communicator, and I have a great voice. People love me, and they love to hear me speak."

Ginger resisted the exercise. She felt she was lying to herself. After convincing her to just go with the flow and repeat the affirmation ten times a day in a mirror (preferably in a bathroom behind closed doors), immediate results were seen and heard within seven days. Her posture had become more erect. The voice (which she had always disliked) was growing more favorable to her.

•**Step 2:** Try to identify the source of the rejection and don't let it define you. Redirect its purpose. No one can stop you from reaching your destiny but you. In Ginger's case, one of her teachers told her she was an ineffective communicator when she was in grade school. She has carried this feedback within her for decades. It was just the beginning of attracting more rejection in her life. When rejection is an expectation, it works as a force to discourage, destroy, and alter one's course in life. The ironic thing is, it can actually be a perception, but to the person who owns it, it's very real.

For example, Kevin Durant goes to the hoops for a layup. Out of nowhere, LeBron James blocks the shot. That's how rejection works in one's life. It literally changes the direction of the expectation—in this case, the two points and the "wow" of the crowd. Unlike Durant who may be fueled by the block, many people internalize rejections and setbacks and allow them to alter their future endeavors. Not Durant—he becomes even more motivated and determined to win the game.

- **Step 3:** In James 4:7 KJV we read these words, "Resist the devil and he will flee from you." God's desire and plan is for us is to prosper as stated in Jeremiah 29:11 NIV. Commit to living life beyond rejection. Say "no" to negative words and old tapes, and don't let them defeat you. Rejection is usually a block, prohibiting one from something greater. Instead reject rejection and unlock limitations in your life. In Ginger's case, this meant getting help to become a more confident communicator.

Body Language

Nonverbal communication has its own voice called body language. It walks, talks, and sends messages. It can show love and even hatred. It can show a person's respect or disrespect for another. This unspoken language carries a voice that can be heard loud and clear; that voice is your spirit.

Nonverbal communication can make or break any form of communicating. It is the reading between the lines when communicating. Actions do speak louder than words, but you must be aware that some body language is universal, and there are unique aspects to certain cultures.

A weak handshake can send the message that a person is shy or has something to hide. A handshake too hard doesn't send a message that one is confident and powerful—quite the opposite actually; it shows the person may be insecure. The balance is a firm handshake. I am asked a lot of questions as to whether women should shake hands. The answer is yes, unless culture is an issue. (More discussion on culture in **Strategy 7, Know Your Audience**.)

Eye contact can't be a miss. It is there or it is not. It is felt when it is inappropriately displayed. Some people have problems looking someone in the eye. That's okay. When you look at a person in the upper part of the bridge of their nose, this is acceptable. Ginger has to redirect her eye contact because she is one of many individuals I categorize as "teeth watchers." The attention goes straight to the mouth. This is common. If you are a teeth watcher, simply look the person you are speaking to in the eye area more often than you are watching their teeth.

If someone has a scar on their face or a body part is exposed, redirect your eye contact and focus on the area mentioned, the upper bridge area between the eyes. When you focus on a negative of an individual, this can force embarrassment on their part and possibly yours.

What's being communicated in each of these sitting positions?

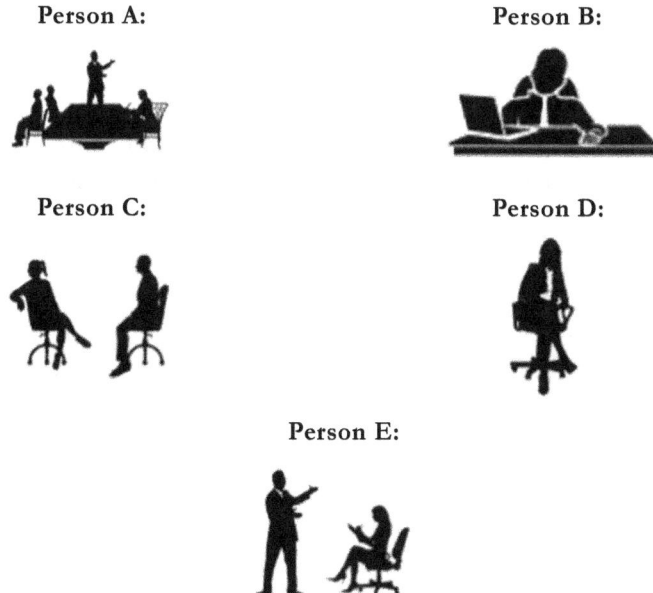

Note: Person A has his back to the presenter, which implies he's not interested. He's definitely not engaged according to this graphic. Person B, is in a slouched position; again, one could read the nonverbal cue as he is unengaged and disinterested. Person C has her shoulder and posturing away from the speaker, another indication of not being engaged. This nonverbal cue says she is not interested in the conversation as her shoulder shifts away. Is there anything wrong with Person D? Years ago, some experts would say "yes" because the crossing of the legs was associated to closed body language. Today, it is a proper and accepted position of sitting. Be aware that people in certain cultures and some religious groups still frown on the idea. Person E, leaning forward indicates she is engaged and interested in who she is listening to. My advice when communicating is to be relaxed. If you are relaxed, you will help calm the person you are speaking to.

There are many wordless messages that communicate. Let's look at a few of them. Dancing, for instance, whether professional or not, is an expression of you, what you are feeling at the time, and your ability or lack of ability to move.

Your home communicates, telling others a lot about the occupant. Text messages, emails, Facebook, Snapchat, and Twitter all send a message about the sender. Your style of dress is also a wordless communicator. When former First Lady Michelle Obama first came out in a sleeveless dress, it was truly a hot topic on talk shows and news programming. Comments were both negative and positive. Many felt this type of attire was inappropriate for the president's wife. Others felt Michelle Obama was communicating that she was her own woman and was not in a box others designed for her. In the meantime, she set a trend, and sleeveless dresses became a staple within the female wardrobe.

Nonverbal messages are also expressed in symbols and sign language. Speaking of Michelle Obama, remember the photo of her giving former President Barack Obama the bump; the media was busy reporting the meaning behind this mysterious clenched fist encounter as many questions were raised as to what it meant.

The bump is like a handshake or a high five to show respect.

Can you identify others?

A:

B:

C:

D:

E:

F:

G:

H:

I:

J:

Did you get them all right? They are in order: A salute—the show of respect for or to a person in military; the Vulcan sign from Star Trek; thumbs up for approval and thumbs down for disapproval; time out, used during games for taking a break; hand kiss, a show of respect; Eskimo kiss, called a kunik, a way to greet and show affection; the cross, a Christian symbol; a queen or person of honor greeting with a royal wave; a vehicle turning right; and the symbol for A-OK, which means everything is all right.

Ginger has challenges with nonverbal cues. Her gestures always fall into a locked position. Her hands are either in her pants pockets or they are clasped behind her back or in front of her. She is very self-conscious. I asked her, "Why do you position your hands like this?" The answer is usually, "I don't know," but in Ginger's case, she replied, "Someone told me to stop moving my hands and body."

What's upsetting about these comments is the individual's action to go to a locked position does not solve the problem. This is not based on anything they are consciously doing. It involves body type, which is correctable and will be explained in more detail in *Strategy 10, Let Your Body Speak*.

Dress for Success

Imagine the CEO of a huge corporation coming out to address employees at their annual employee meeting. He appears to be slightly unkempt. He was in need of a haircut three or four weeks ago. He's wearing torn jeans that are too tight and a button-down shirt. Mr. French addresses the group, but little is learned about what he is saying because the attention is on his attire and his lack of appropriateness.
What you wear speaks volumes. The rule I set is to dress at least one notch above your audience when presenting. In the case of the CEO, his audience members were all professionally dressed. They were stunned at his appearance. Their minds could not stay focused on his words and instead focused on his clothing.

Ginger has a concern in this area. As a technician, she was allowed to wear very casual clothing. Dress down was considered okay because she worked behind the scenes. Outside of work, this would also be her normal attire, jeans and a shirt or sweater.

Now, she is being asked to speak to corporate executives. Should she wear a dress, a skirt set, or a pantsuit? Ginger wondered what happened to just wearing nice slacks and a shirt. Besides the question of what she should wear, she had to decide on the color. The answers can only be determined after "doing your homework." Find out some background information on the group you are addressing. How do they dress? Are they polished professionals or casual? Are they men or are there women in this group? If there are women, what do they normally wear?

After researching, Ginger had a decision to make. Research revealed that there are two women in the group, and they always wear pantsuits. The personalities within the group are both a mixture of stern and friendly, but mostly serious and stern. She also found out that the group normally wears black when they meet.

What Ginger chose to wear might surprise you. It would have been easy for her to hide behind black, but instead she wore a royal blue suit. She chose to wear a skirt instead of pants. The reason for her choice was fairly obvious: Ginger was introducing change to the company. After discussing the research, we felt it was appropriate to introduce it to the board members at the onset. We wanted the first impression to be professionalism and that she had something exciting lurking on the corporation's horizon.

Black or navy would have also been good choices, but in this case, the colors would have said, "I'm trying to fit in," when that was not the message Ginger needed to present.

Diet: What Not to Eat before a Speech

What you eat or drink can make a difference in how you speak. If you don't believe me, before your next presentation, drink a soda. Chances are, you are sure to belch. In most communication books, the issue of food is usually not mentioned. What you eat or drink prior to speaking can destroy your performance. I have produced a variety of television programs and speak for events.

One day while speaking, my mouth gummed up after drinking extremely cold water. It was as if you were watching an out-of-sync movie. My voice was saying one thing, and my lips spoke another. For a healthy speaking experience, here is a list of do's and don'ts to consider before speaking:

What you eat or drink prior can destroy your performance.

Do not
1. Drink carbonated beverages
2. Eat spicy foods
3. Eat turkey
4. Fill your drinking glass with cold water
5. Overeat

Do
1. Drink warm or room temperature water
2. Eat anything within reason that is not on the don't list
3. Eat small portions
4. When in doubt of what to eat, enjoy fruits and vegetables, but avoid spicy foods

Let's examine carbonated beverages. They can cause one to belch not once, but continuously. I've tested this theory by giving speakers both carbonated and noncarbonated beverages before they spoke. The speakers drinking carbonated beverages all belched at some point in their presentation. If you want to drink something, drink warm or room temperature water.

If turkey is on the menu and you are speaking at an engagement, avoid eating it since turkey is said to contain an amino acid called tryptophan. While this is a controversial subject matter among researchers as to whether or not turkey really does make us sleepy, don't chance it! One group says yes because turkey does contain tryptophan, which is a natural sedative. They say tryptophan helps the body produce niacin, which helps produce serotonin. This chemical acts as a calming agent in the brain and plays a key role in sleep. Another group disagrees and says that turkey's tryptophan only affects a person if eaten on an empty stomach.

I have personally seen audiences yawn more after a turkey lunch. It is a good idea to see what your audience is having for lunch. If you are speaking in the afternoon right after eating, you may have to push a little harder to keep everyone's attention, particularly if turkey was the choice for lunch.

Spicy foods can also cause an adverse effect and reaction on both sides of the microphone. Some people can handle spicy foods and do not have a reaction, while others may belch or have an increased urge to run to the bathroom due to diarrhea. Spicy foods or acidic foods can irritate the intestines. If there is an opportunity to make a food choice, avoid meals that can affect your audience; keep them bland. My personal rule of thumb regarding the presenter is to eat after speaking. Why take chances? If you must eat beforehand, keep it very light and bland.

Mental Prep

They keep coming and coming. They are usually always negative. They keep you down. They seek to destroy you. They are the voices. In Ginger's case, they constantly remind her that she will bomb her presentation. When she looks in the mirror, they tell her she is a failure. As she is exercising (which by the way she has lost seven pounds), they tell her that she is doing the exercises for nothing, they are a waste of time, and the physical routines will not help her because she is a terrible speaker. Unfortunately, Ginger internalizes the voices.

Negative voices come directly from satan. Ginger believes them because the words are similar to what her grade school teacher told her when she was attempting to deliver a speech. They are the same type of words with the same pain that a family member spoke to her when she was growing up.

It is not uncommon for these words to creep up to destroy and rob one's self-esteem. However, you must know you have the power to stop the words. Here is how I suggest you go about it:

1. **Think positive.** When the voices start, talk back to them with positive words. If the voice says, "You can't sing that song; you are going to hit all the wrong notes," speak back and say, "I can do all things through Christ who strengthens me" (Philippians 4:13)—and that includes singing the song. Say the opposite.

2. **Design affirmations** and say them at least ten times a day. Look into the mirror and say, "I am beautiful/handsome. People love to be around me and love to listen to me." Another one to say is this: "I am healthy, happy, successful, loving, and prosperous." Affirmations go into the spirit of the person to rid negativity. This is a sure way to take control over negative influences. The key is to say them in a closed setting (perhaps in your car, a bathroom, etc.) and repeat them out loud and aggressively each time. Your self-esteem will improve! The negative subconscious voices will go away. I have lots of clients who can attest to this. The Bible says in James 4:7, if you resist the devil and don't give in, he will flee.

3. **Motivate Yourself.** Find a good speaker who motivates you to create positively. Listen to him or her. Your motivator may even be a good friend. If you happen to not have something or someone who motivates you to think positive about yourself, then play a song that makes you feel good. I have several, but there is one that makes me feel I can accomplish anything. It is entitled "Believe in Yourself" by Lena Horne. Feel free to borrow my song until you find one of your own.

Spiritual Prep

Fear (also known in this case as the devil) rears its ugly head often whenever one takes a stand to speak positive words. There is a difference between feeling nervous and being fearful. Nervousness comes and goes. We'll talk more about nervousness and how to overcome it in the communication clinic portion at the end of this book. Fear can be crippling. Fear is designed to destroy one's spirit and will. To rid fear at its roots, it is important to speak to it with your mouth and spirit.

By confessing Scriptures, you gain control. Try it:

> **2 Timothy 1:7**—"For God has not given us a spirit of fear, but of power and of love and of a sound mind."

> **Luke 10:19 NIV**—"I have given you authority to trample on snakes and scorpions and to overcome all the power of the enemy; nothing will harm you."

> **Philippians 4:13**—"I can do all things through Christ who strengthens me."
> Repeat these ten times daily. You have to know who you are in God's eyes. By internalizing these Scriptures, you will be released from the quicksand of fear that wants to suffocate you and drag you down.

Most of us go to our physician to get a medical examination once a year. There is another exam in which we should consider—a personal assessment—where we evaluate ourselves physically, mentally, and spiritually. We have to be prepared for any assignment or opportunity in our future. 'For I know the plans I have for you,' declares the Lord" (Jeremiah 29:11). Our job is to be ready.

Challenge

Identify ways you can prepare your body for communication success. What steps do you need to take physically, mentally, and spiritually to improve your skills?

Declaration

I am beautiful/handsome! I am a great communicator, and I have a great voice. People love to hear me speak. I see myself as God sees me. I am free from fear and anxiety. I am confident and I'm awesome!

- Strategy 5 -
PREPARE YOUR MATERIALS

> **Let all things be done decently and in order.**
> 1 Corinthians 14:40, New King James Version

Communication is important to God, which is one of the reasons why we have the Holy Bible today as a guide to knowing His will for our lives. "God is not the author of confusion but of peace" (1 Corinthians 14:33). As the people of Corinth struggled with chaos within the church, it was the Apostle Paul who told them to get their house in order. God does things decently and in order and expects the same from us. That being said, let's look at the elements of preparing your materials.

What's Your Point?

As we learned in Strategy 1, purpose is foundational. Purpose gives direction to communication. Without it, your audience can get lost, become confused, or totally lose interest in what you are trying to communicate. Once you determine your purpose, the rest will follow. Before preparing your materials, make sure you first determine the purpose or point of your presentation by answering these questions:

- What do you want the people to learn?
- What tone do you want to set for the communication: serious, humorous, or conversational?
- What points do you want to emphasize and reinforce? What are you selling?
- What tools will be used to help you drive home the major message?

- What will be the length of the presentation?
- Do you want to educate or simply be informative?

Organize Your Materials

Next, organize your materials. Organization can be challenging when preparing for communication. If your presentation is structured incorrectly, the goal of the actual presentation can get lost and end in chaos.

When preparing for talk shows, I have found that you have to know what you are talking about and with whom you are talking. Before going on air, I spend time investigating the topic of discussion as well as talking to the guests to gain insight into their stories. Research is key. If you examine what makes a good television show or a memorable presentation, it almost always comes down to the prep and research.

Emotionally, this stage of the process can be difficult for some and overwhelming for others. New ideas can come from many directions. It's challenging because what you are dealing with is disorganized chaos. However, use your purpose as your compass, and you will be able to steer your ideas in the right direction. Here's how to achieve this goal:

Ginger's anxiety escalated to another level when she thought about pulling her presentation together. I outlined the following tips for her to keep her calm and focused, and I'm sure they will help you, too.

Preparation Tip 1—The 5 W's and 1 H

Include the 5 W's: Who, What, When, Where, and Why in every presentation. These five helped her organize. Who, What, When, Where, and Why are journalistic tools used to build stories. There is one additional tool that must be considered and that is how! How are changes going to happen or how will this help? What will be the springboard or beginning step for this new idea rolling? These tools can also be utilized to help build focus to presentations.

The Presentation	The Content:
Who is your audience?	**Who** will be involved in making this project a success?
What is your purpose?	**What** content information are you trying to deliver?
When will this happen?	**When** will the project launch?
Where will this happen?	**Where** should this project begin?
Why should it happen?	**Why** is this project essential or necessary now?
How must it happen?	**How** will this project improve the company or situation?

Just like determining the purpose of your presentation, using the five W's and one H helps you create an organized structure and squelches your anxiety. A clearer picture starts to form, and your materials will come together.

When Ginger answered the *who* questions, she learned more information about her audience and what they were expecting from her. The *what* question provided her with answers she needed to gain more of a focus on what she was presenting. Remember, Ginger developed her plan for the company. You would think organizing and writing would be easy, but no. Selling an idea or product takes creativity, connection with your audience, a clear plan, incorporation of technology, and corresponding verbal and nonverbal communication.

Answering the *when* question provided answers about the time of day of the presentation. She found out it was scheduled for 8 a.m. Ginger was pleased because she is a morning person. The where gave her the location. The why question was something she always knew. It gave her comfort. She knew why the company should listen to her. The how started her head spinning because she didn't know how to take the concept out of her head, put it on paper, and polish the presentation well enough to sell her audience. That is where good research comes into play.

Research

Become an expert on your subject matter. Pull together everything you can on the subject matter you are presenting. This involves checking the Internet, books, conducting personal interviews, finding documented case studies, and including your own personal experience with the subject. Read, read, and read! Consume yourself in the knowledge of your topic.

"Where do I begin?" That is the most-asked question when it comes to putting together a presentation. Ideas fly in and out of your head, and soon it's spinning. People generally become consumed, fearing the worst and procrastinating as much as possible. The best advice I can give you is to confront this problem. It is not going away.

You must fight the number one enemy of success—*procrastination*. This common enemy comes to swallow us up like quicksand. I've actually had people brag to me about being a procrastinator. What they are really saying is, they own the act of putting off anything they don't want to deal with. Procrastinators flunk out of schools, lose jobs, fail at marriage, and even avoid living life to the fullest. The best way to fight procrastination is to attack and deal with whatever you are putting off, even if it hurts. As you make a decision to pursue the undesired and actually put action to the plan, you are moving in the right direction to combat the problem. If you don't, this flaw will destroy your dreams and endeavors. Each battle won against procrastination decreases its strength. The key is to keep fighting.

You must fight the number one enemy of success—procrastination.

Construct the Puzzle

1. Visualize a jigsaw puzzle, not one with 1000 tiny pieces, but one containing up to ten components. Putting together a ten-piece puzzle is a lot easier than trying to connect a thousand pieces. The picture becomes clearer with fewer pieces to connect.

2. Name and label your puzzle pieces. They represent outline topics for your presentation. For example: Ginger has taken her research information and categorized it into five areas to cover. She then sorts her research into these five areas. At this point, the categories are all filled with literature that may or may not be used.

3. Examine each puzzle segment or outline point, one at a time. Decipher what information is relevant or not. After sorting, the vision of the presentation becomes less complicated.

Visuals

The biggest mistake one can make is to stand before a group of people, present information verbally, and expect everyone to buy into the sell. The verbal part is a key component to sell, but it is not the only way people buy in or learn. Thirty percent of the general population consists of auditory learners, while sixty-five percent are visual and need to see what they are learning. Experts say women tend to be more visual and men more kinesthetic. When preparing a presentation, all learning styles must be considered when addressing any audience.

Technology is a tool that has been proven helpful in increasing learning capabilities. Schools across the country have integrated advanced computer animation to challenge students. So, how do you marry words and technology into a happy relationship?

- **Rule1:** Use technology in the presentation. Overheads and flip charts were popular in the twentieth century. Even though they still have purpose, there are other options. You are in the twenty-first century, use twenty-first century technology.

- **Rule 2:** Be creative. Feel free to tell your story with animated works.

- **Rule 3:** Do not write out your presentation for the audience to read it. This technology does not enhance your presentation. Bullet points or a list of main ideas can be applied here.

- **Rule 4:** Limit content to one idea per page or visual. One of the biggest mistakes made is overcrowding to fill a whole page with information.

- **Rule 5:** If you are writing words, make sure they are big enough for your audience to read. Don't make people squint. Some companies today are asking employees to use at least a 24-point font.

- **Rule 6:** Use appropriate colors. Keep in mind that members of your audience may be color blind. Internet studies show that five to eight percent of men and a half percent of women are color blind, which equates to approximately one in twelve males and one in every two hundred females. The male is said to inherit the disorder from his mother, who is usually not color blind. Most color-confused people can't tell the difference between green and red. Another design component to avoid is using bold, offensive colors. Blue, black, dark purple, dark green, dark burgundy, and dark brown are generally safe. Yellow and light gray are hard to see and should not be used. Remember, colors such as red and orange are sometimes good to emphasize certain points, and they can be used to enhance a visual. Standing alone, words in red or orange are often hard to read.

- **Rule 7:** Simplify your creation. Don't make it so fancy it distracts from your verbal communication. Let your words and the visual work together. There are a number of technological enhancers available to make any presentation sparkle and shine.

Tools to Enhance Presentations

A. If your audience is in a room and it is hard for people in all areas of the room to see you, make sure viewing monitors of appropriate size are in place.

B. For visuals, it is good to use Keynote, Prezi or PowerPoint for presentations. Text, charts, graphs, images, animation, sound effects, and even music can all be integrated to enhance presentations.

C. Live 3D models specifically designed to display a finished project are always good to show audiences. Make sure the image can be seen by everyone.

D. Video segments can be used to add emphasis. They can consist of brief interviews, animation, or actual scenes.

E. Print material still has its place in the visual world. Handouts are always good, but they must follow the guidelines of rules for visuals.

F. Live interactions via Skype and other media can work to enhance presentations. Make sure you test connections on both ends to make sure they are working properly. Always have a Plan B just in case there is a technical problem.

The bottom line when choosing visuals for your presentation comes with asking yourself the following questions:
- Does the visual add value to the point being made?
- Is the visual well-constructed?
- Does the visual boost learning?

If the answer is "no" to any of these, eliminate the visual or reconstruct it until it meets the criteria. Visuals, if applied and presented properly, will support the credibility of the presenter as well as the presentation.

Building Your Masterpiece into Presentation Style

Ginger has created her outline and knows what information and examples acquired from her research will be used in her presentation. She has also investigated and figured out what technology she will be using. The challenging part for her now is putting the presentation together.

The best presentation or speech is one that moves and flows. A speech should not put someone to sleep but, rather spark interest and engage the listener. First impressions for any type of communication should be positive. The first encounter with others tells a story of what to expect from a person's communication and what is in their heart. Negative body language can result in a negative first impression, so strive to leave a great impression.

Preparing a Presentation

The following decisions must be made when preparing a presentation:

- **Decision 1:** How can I begin powerfully? Make the decision to be powerful in your approach. The beginning of one's presentation can include telling a story, painting a scenario, telling a joke, using a quote, or stating a statistic. Think of yourself as a television show; will you be watched, or will people switch to another channel?

> **Think of yourself as a television show; will you be watched, or will people switch to another channel?**

- **Decision 2:** How can I creatively weave in the points I am trying to make without saying the same words over and over? One can do this effectively by using visuals and recontextualization. "By implementing our plan for alternative energy (display graphic), the result is a drastic price reduction for the consumer." One could also repeat the point by saying, "Everyday people like you and me will save money with this plan in place."

- **Decision 3:** How can I involve my audience in my presentation? This can happen by engaging in a question–answer segment, allowing for feedback during the presentation, using audience members in role-play situations, calling the name of an individual or two when making a point, and/or utilizing experts in the audience to drive a point home. Be cautious not to single out too many people in your audience; this can be a distraction and can also put people on edge.

•**Decision 4:** How can I keep my audience's attention? You can motivate people to be intrigued with your presentation. Keep your energy level up. Come out of yourself and be an entertainer. We all don't feel one hundred percent all the time. Sometimes we have to rise up to the occasion to get a job done well and effectively.

•**Decision 5:** How can I end my presentation successfully? When nearing the end, never take on the attitude of it's over; now I can relax. You have fought hard to make the presentation a success; fight even harder to give it a memorable and powerful ending.

Suggestions: Just like in the beginning, you can tell a story, use a quote, state a statistic, repeat vital information, paint a picture of an outcome (don't forget your visual if it is relevant), and if you can effectively use humor, go ahead and make them laugh. These are all acceptable means for concluding a presentation. The end of your presentation should leave a lasting impression called the "wow effect," which simply means, you've made a favorable impact on your audience.

Write Your Speech/Presentation

Now, it is time to write your speech or presentation. Here are some tips to follow:

1. Think and write conversationally. Newspapers are said to be written on an eighth-grade reading level. It is a natural instinct to want to impress your audience. It is okay to use some big words, depending on your audience, but they should never be used to belittle anyone. The goal is for them to understand the presentation. Those grandiose and pretentious words could ultimately leave them missing the most important points of your presentation.

2. Construct the communication in the order in which you will be speaking; it must have a flow. Don't skip around.

3. Keep it simple. Relax. The goal is to sail smoothly through the presentation and fulfill your purpose, not to send the audience on a

rollercoaster ride.

4. Let your visuals help you. Allow them to emphasize important information. If you use Keynote or PowerPoint, you can create a cheat sheet, describing your graphics to help you deliver technical or challenging information they are not privy to.

5. Keep your audience in mind. Write to their level and involve them when you can.

6. Write and rewrite. Rewriting is a great learning experience. It helps you know your subject matter even better. It is not necessary to write every word you are going to say, but it is important to write down challenging material you need to memorize or say verbatim. Be credible when trying to tell something from memory. It is okay to pick up a note card to read pertinent information if that is what it takes to deliver the information correctly.

When writing, if you get to a point where you think you cannot write, just start writing! Put on some motivational music. Then, just start writing in segments. Start with an easy section; then move on. Soon, you will have the speech or presentation outlined or written.

Next, we'll add what I call the secret weapon to any presentation. It is the reason why a book becomes a best seller and why people like to connect to certain speakers. You can look at it as the sugar in a cake recipe. If it is missing, the whole cake flops. It is called emotion. It is the difference between telling a story and telling it well. We all know emotions involve an expression or display of happiness, sadness, anger, excitement, and so on. The best way to add emotion is to write using words to express the feeling of the person or situation. Be descriptive, but don't overdo it.

In the movie *Red Tails*, George Lucas introduces us to a character named Lightning. Lucas allows us to experience a little of his world by painting the picture on the big screen. Lightning is a daredevil pilot with the Tuskegee Airmen known for his confidence, who loves being a pilot fighting for his country. One day while coming back from a mission in Italy, his eye catches a woman while she is outside her home. He pursued her, and the two fell in love even though they didn't speak the same language. What George Lucas allows the audience to feel is the romance between the couple. Lightning proposes to the Italian woman, and they eventually agree to marry.

Unfortunately, Lightning doesn't make it back from his last mission. He is shot, and his plane crashes. While holding her photo, his last words are for Sophia, telling her he loves her and is sorry.

The appropriate way to inject the human element of emotion into a movie, conversation, or a presentation is to tell a great story by putting yourself into the situation.

Tell the Story

Ginger, like many people, struggles telling stories. How do you tell a great story? How do you keep your audiences' attention? What stories do you choose to tell? Should they be funny? How do you integrate a story into your presentation? When creating a story, use words that will create a vivid image of the scene you are painting in the minds of your audience. Stories are impactful, and people remember them. I have selected four experts who are great in this area and offer advice to master the art of storytelling.

A big part of TV personality Sonya Gavankar's job is storytelling. When she tells a story, all eyes are on her, sometimes in disbelief. She has a way of combining body language and words into a dramatic presentation that keeps her audiences wanting more. Sonya, a filmmaker, television and podcast host, and social content creator has been seen on ABC and CBS affiliates, PBS, QVC, and even the Puppy Bowl. Sonya was also a TV correspondent and public relations manager for Newseum and Freedom Forum in Washington, DC. She offers this advice to improve your storytelling ability:

- Turn your words into stories for you to perform.
- Words should feel yummy in your mouth.
- Be authentic. Your story should reflect your personal ethos.
- Listen before you speak.
- Know who you are and why you deserve to be giving this message.
- Know your audience.

Our next expert is named "The Storyteller" and has inspired and motivated thousands. He has a unique way of combining humor and fact into contagious dialogue. James Ford offers the following tips to keep audiences wanting more:

- Have something to say and make a point.
- Learn how to say it well.
- Learn how to be brief.
- Learn how to read your audience.

James Ford says, "What makes a story so apropos is to make it believable. The formula: the reason why people laugh at comedians is they tell a story, present it well and allow the audience to become comfortable. Then there is an unexpected shift that causes laughter. This creates an opportunity to drive a point."

Here is a story he tells before a motivational talk: "There was a man who dialed 911. The man on the other end asked, what is your emergency? He said my emergency is I have two women fighting over me. The man on the other end said, let me get this straight. Your emergency is you have two women fighting over you; why do you consider this a problem? He said, man, the ugly one is winning." That draws laughter and loosens up the audience. James Ford goes on to say, "This is the problem with most of you. You allow the ugly to get the upper hand. Don't let the ugly win in your life."

Our third expert is a business and wealth developer, James Dentley, who sponsors a professional speakers' camp and bureau. He has trained over 700,000 people in business and has personally created over eighty millionaires by using his proven success strategies. He knows the importance of telling a story and telling it well. He has captured the attention of his audiences from around the world and has kept them wanting more by creating an experience worth talking about. Here are tips from sought-after speaker James Dentley:

- Keep a journal. A life worth living is worth recording.

- Know that your life matters. Everything you do or don't do impacts the lives of other people.

- Look for the lesson in everything and collect stories from everyone you meet.

- Use your imagination. All of our life experiences are anchored in stories from Dr. Seuss to every song and movie we have ever seen or heard—all are based on telling a story.

- Read! Read! Read! Read books, watch YouTube videos, and collect stories from others. Remember, make a point with a story and tell a story to make a point! There is power in your story!

Les Brown, renowned motivational expert, author, and television personality had this to say about storytelling during a PR opportunity I set up for him at a television station:

- The key to effective communication is being able to relate to the person you are talking to.

- Don't let what you want to say get in the way of what the person needs to hear. You must learn something about that audience to be able to relate to them, and to communicate and to create a level of identification.

- Use stories for the purpose of distracting, disputing, and inspiring. How people live their lives is a result of the story they believe about themselves.

- When you are an effective communicator, you distract them from their story, and through the values and things you believe in, you are to create a shift in their thinking and inspire them to make new choices after they leave your presence.

We all have a story to tell, whether it is told verbally or nonverbally.

For instance, a protest emerged through downtown Chicago. People were waving signs opposing the violence in their city. From January through August, 2016, 425 people were killed, and 2,800 people had been shot. Hundreds protested over a concern that their city was not safe, and they wanted this violence to end.

Onlookers were silenced by a story that rolled out right before their eyes. They had heard about protesters going to the streets on the news, but now this scene was a reality. The impact of this story was told visually and was emotionally felt by those who witnessed the march.

Bring your story alive by injecting emotion so it will be felt. A story can be humorous or dramatic and contain a sad or happy ending. When relating and telling a story, own it, tell it in your personal style and leave a lasting and memorable impression. A great example of a person who mastered this concept is Steve Jobs. He believed in and understood the great product he created and marketed. Jobs amplified Apple's voice, and he managed to get the world to tell his story.

Challenge

It's time to practice! Prepare a presentation for a group of high-level executives in your field of interest. Using concepts presented in this strategy, what steps were the easiest for you? Which were the most difficult? What new ideas will you add to your presentation? Create a story using concepts mentioned in this strategy.

Declaration

I am organized. I am productive. I am emotionally healthy, and I breathe life into my writing. I am a great presenter, and I am a great storyteller.

- Strategy 6 -

Understand Your Environment

> **My child, don't lose sight of common sense and discernment. Hang on to them, for they will refresh your soul. They are like jewels on a necklace.**
> Proverbs 3:21–22, New Living Translation

Before God's chosen people moved into the land that we know today as Israel, Moses sent twelve men there to spy and understand the environment they would soon occupy. He gave them specific instructions about what to look for and told them to report what they learned, so the people could best prepare for the move. Moses gave the men these instructions as he sent them out to explore the land:

Go north through the Negev into the hill country. See what the land is like, and find out whether the people living there are strong or weak, few or many. See what kind of land they live in. Is it good or bad? Do their towns have walls, or are they unprotected like open camps? Is the soil fertile or poor? Are there many trees? Do your best to bring back samples of the crops you see. (Numbers 13:17– 20, NLT)

To prepare for a presentation, I highly recommend that you endeavor to be as thorough as Moses was and learn as much as possible about the environment in which you will be speaking. Trust me; the more you know about your environment before you arrive, the more likely you are to avoid many of the obstacles that can make or break your presentation. Below are some specifics to consider.

Why Is Environment So Important?

Environment plays a major role in the success of one's presentation. It's not only the environment, but your reaction to the environment that matters. Just to give you an example, a while back, I was forced to find another gym for my workouts. My exercise partner and I have always worked well together. Our gym closed, forcing us to find another location. My spirit did not connect to this new gym because it felt and looked cold. The people working there seemed to have a less-than-friendly attitude and approach. For weeks, I tried to connect and give the place a chance. I later had a conversation with my fitness coach, who went to another gym after the closing, and I expressed my feelings to him. He immediately told me that if my spirit was not comfortable, it would be better to leave and find another place where I wouldn't feel stressed. I did, and I joined a gym where I now feel calm and relaxed. It's warm, and the people are friendlier. Unfortunately, my workout partner and I went separate ways for awhile. Occasionally, we get together and work out at the gym where I belong, and eventually he joined my gym.

Environments communicate. The message may be positive or negative. Have you ever walked into someone's home or office and not wanted to leave? What you were feeling was the spirit of that room or home. This is usually a warm environment where you feel comfortable and relaxed. On the other hand, there are environments that scream the opposite. In the case of the gym, the spirit of the facility felt cold and uninviting. My focus was off, and I could not concentrate on what I needed to do.

Environments communicate.

When delivering a presentation, always do your homework. Check out the room (if possible) at least a day before you get up and speak. It is a major part of your prep. There are three main components to communication: you, your environment, and your audience. If your environment is not conducive to your success, this can be a real problem. Let's examine how our five senses play a part in how we react to our surroundings.

Sight: Location Aesthetics, Size, and Setup

What the naked eye sees in a room can determine whether an individual accepts or rejects an environment. There are several components that make up the decision.

1. **Room Size:** Is the room too small or too large? Is it conducive to meeting the needs of the presenter? Room size is crucial to a person who is claustrophobic. Those who suffer with claustrophobia make up fifteen to thirty-seven percent of the world's population. The fear of being in a room that is too small can spark feelings of having no escape or being closed in. Just by walking into a room, a person who is claustrophobic may feel anxious. If this happens, the person will look around to see what is making them feel uncomfortable. It could be the lack of windows in the room or the temperature of the room. One thing you must understand is that people with this disorder don't have a lot of faith that doors will operate as they should. In their minds, the doors of washrooms, elevators, or any room can lock them into a confined space. Claustrophobics love nonrestrictive environments and like to be able to maneuver and leave the room when they are ready to go. This is quite the opposite for smaller percentage of people who are diagnosed with claustrophilia (the love of closed, tight places with the windows and doors shut). It is not uncommon for a claustrophile to enjoy being in a cage-like atmosphere.

2. **Room Color:** Are the colors soothing? Are they coordinated? Are they distracting? Colors are present throughout a room, from the paint on the walls and the carpet on the floor to the furniture. Soothing colors help reduce stress. Serene, cool colors such

as blues, greens, and purples as well as pale, pastel colors such as yellow, sand, and beige are used to calm emotions. Neon colors, depending on how they are used, can have the opposite effect. Bright orange, red, and turquoise are used as stimulants.

3. **Room Setup:** Is the room arranged in a favorable way for the audience and presenter? Is the equipment placed in an appropriate area, so it is easily accessible to the presenter? The room setup can be one that is conducive or negative. Seating should be arranged so that all participants can see the speaker. There may be only chairs or both tables and chairs.

Let's examine this diagram.

Please indicate the appropriate areas to sit if you are trying to create a nonthreatening atmosphere.

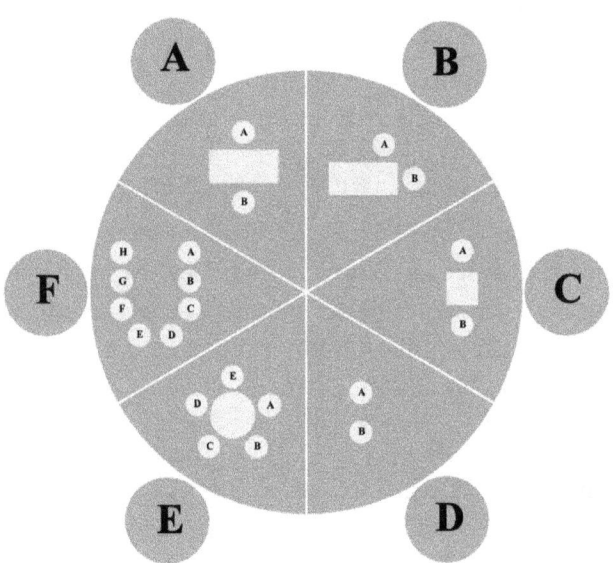

In A, it is better to swing the chair to the other side of the table as shown in B. In C, remove the table to look like D. In example E, it doesn't matter where you sit because all sides are equal. The goal is to avoid setting up a power position that sends a message, "I am in charge." In F, it is better to sit along the sides in the middle to be inclusive, instead of at the head table. This head position should only be taken if an organization insists you occupy that particular seat. If not, sit among the people with whom you are meeting. If you have a problem seeing everyone, slightly pull your chair from the table.

4. **Technical Equipment Placement:** It is also important where the technical equipment is placed in the room. It should be positioned so that it is user friendly for the presenter and in an appropriate place for the audience to view audio-visual displays. This should be pre-arranged prior to the actual presentation.

5. **Clutter:** Is the room neat? While some people are not bothered by clutter, there are others who are very disturbed by anything that is out of place. Such clutter sends an uneasy feeling through their bodies. A dirty atmosphere, an environment with torn drapes, or an overflowing garbage can also send the same uncomfortable feeling. If needed, unclutter your environment.

6. **Lighting:** Is the light too bright or too dim? Are some of the light bulbs burned out? Do you have control over the lighting? Lighting adds life to a room. If it's too dim, you'll know it, and so will your audience. If it's overly bright, you will know that, too. If natural light from the sun is beaming in through windows inappropriately, this can be an annoyance for the speaker or audience. The idea is to be able to have some control over lighting so that it can be dimmed or turned on or off when necessary. The lighting situation should also be one that is comfortable for everyone.

Sound: Acoustics, Noises, and Distractions

Unless you are walking into a soundproof room, there are various sounds within any environment that can help or hinder a presentation.

1. **Natural Sounds**: Are the room sounds unbearable? Can you control them? Do you need to request another room? Every room has its own sounds, and most will be out of your control: lights will buzz, ventilation carries its own beat, and technical equipment whispers its own tune. Nature speaks as well, and you may have to deal with rain, crickets chirping, cicadas, rivers flowing, thunderstorms, traffic, the wind, or airplanes. These sounds can produce even more challenges when you're making your presentation. If natural sounds in a room are unbearable, steps should be taken to minimize them prior to the delivery of the actual presentation.

2. **Audio:** How is the sound controlled? Are you responsible for monitoring your own sound level? How do you connect your iPod or smartphone to existing audio equipment? Piped-in music may be a standard for the facility hosting your planned event. Make sure the music is turned off in your area before you present. Add this to your to-do list when visiting the room before the event. Also, make sure that if you have planned music or sound effects that it works with the sound system in the room. Find a contact that you can rely on to help you with audio. While on-site in the room, check the microphone set-up. Make a choice as to what type of microphone is comfortable for you. If you need to have a more hands-free approach, perhaps a lavalier (wireless microphone) is best. Do you feel more comfortable with a hand-held microphone? If so, the choice is a wireless or a wired microphone. Wireless allows more freedom for you to roam around the room. Perform a

microphone check—yes, even if it is the day before; and of course, follow up and have the levels adjusted the day of the event. Checking for levels ahead of time can provide knowledge of system problems such as the sound being muffled or it just not working properly.

3. **Distraction:** Is there anything you can do to prevent or minimize distractions? When scouting out a room, it is also important to be aware of building sounds. Air conditioning, heating, ventilation knocks from malfunctions in the system, or a squeaky door are all sounds that may cause distractions when presenting. The key is awareness. A simple consultation with the engineer of a building can help minimize, and in some cases eliminate, unwanted building sounds. A major concern in many facilities is fighting the noise overflow from other meetings. Walls between you and the next presenter can be thin, so weak that both functions can be heard on both sides of the walls. It is very distracting when music overrides your verbal meeting. Know what is happening in your room area ahead of time. If there is a celebration in Meeting Room A, and you are in scheduled to present in Meeting Room B with just an adjoining wall between the two, a better choice for a room may be Meeting Room D in another wing.

Taste: Food and Beverages

Know what food and/or beverages will be in your environment. Connecting with catering or your contact person to know what time you can expect the audience's entree delivered to the room will keep you on your game plan. A planned distraction is better managed than an unexpected surprise. This will also help you plan your breaks. Make sure food brought into the room is not against the cultural or religious beliefs of the audience (See more on culture in **Strategy 7**).

Smell: Aromas and Odors

Smells can be received as positive or negative. Odors offensive to some people are not necessarily offensive to others. The perception is based on personal exposure, opinions, and experiences.

> 1. **Types of Odors:** Pleasant and unpleasant aromas are all around us in any unprotected environment. Some common ones are trash can odors, food, unsanitary debris outside a building, oxides of sulfur, nitrogen ozone, increased carbon dioxide levels, and other chemical odors.
>
> 2. **Unexpected Odors**: Odors may be a part of the environment, but they can also be added to an environment. People who smoke can add a negative foulness to the air. Cigarette smoke can be very annoying and unpleasant to nonsmokers. Another scent that can be brought into a room is body odor. Mustiness or a stench that exemplify uncleanness will distract the attention from the presenter.
>
> 3. **Effects on Audience:** Odors can distract an audience. The attention span of the group can be diverted by smells that are unpleasant. Reactions can be mild to severe such as itchy, watery, or burning eyes, skin rashes or irritations, headaches, nausea, and nose/throat irritations that may result from allergens or chemical fumes.

Odors that can be eliminated should be dealt with before the presentation. For instance, Ginger knew fish was going to be served before her presentation. She is allergic to fish and asked her contact person to please change the menu, if possible, because she can't smell or eat it without having a major reaction. If possible, determine the source or cause of any bad odors and eliminate them as soon as you can, prior to your event. The goal is to have a clean environment that is not offensive to anyone. It is hard to determine whether loud perfumes or a distinctive smell in the form of body odor will walk into your environment. Some people can't control their scent. The effect is based on the sensitivity and reaction of those around them. Not all odors emitted into a room are preventable. Control what can be controlled. Exercise the freedom necessary to make your environment clean.

Touch: Comfort, Proximity, Safety, and Courtesy

When scouting out your environment, work to make it as safe, comfortable, and pleasant for all involved. You need to be comfortable in the area where you are speaking and have close proximity to your equipment, materials, and resources. Likewise, you need to maintain a respect for your host and the environment you will be using for your presentation.

Comfort and proximity are major considerations. Is the equipment in the proper places for your comfort? Can you maneuver and access its controls? If you are using a remote, is it in a user-friendly place? Do you need to control the lights? Learn how before the presentation or assign someone to operate lighting if it is awkward or difficult for you. Do you have everything you need in place? Is your positioning to the audience right for you? Your instincts will tell you if you need to move the podium or the lectern or not use it at all. Most preachers and teachers are more effective with lecterns.

Safety and courtesy are foundational to every presentation. Always remember that you are a guest on someone else's turf. Be courteous and respectful. Don't try to go in and make drastic changes unless absolutely necessary. If there are changes you want to make, explain your concern to the host and allow them to make the changes. Your instincts will tell you when an environment feels warm and comfortable, just like they scream when a room is cold and dysfunctional. By examining your environment through your five senses, you will gain a great deal of knowledge about the area to help you function effectively within the unexpected.

> **Always remember that you are a guest on someone else's turf.**

Challenge

How can you make your environment comfortable and workable for your purpose or for your audience? What changes or things do you need to put on your to-do list before you speak? If the unexpected occurs, how will you stay focused? What is your plan A and plan B?

Declaration

I am in control when the unexpected happens.

- Strategy 7 -

KNOW YOUR AUDIENCE

> **I, Wisdom, live together with good judgment. I know where to discover knowledge and discernment.**
> Proverbs 8:12, New Living Translation

Applause! Applause! Applause! It's what every presenter hopes to hear and feel at the end of an event, speech, or even one-on-one communication. Hand clapping, in most instances, indicates the presentation or talk was well received. It may not be appropriate in some settings to clap, but every presenter would like to feel the sense behind the applause—the acceptance. The goal for any presenter is to deliver sound material in a positive manner, to win over the audience, and wow them.

How do I impress my audience? First of all, let's turn the tables. Place yourself in the audience of a movie or theater setting. What are your expectations? Do you want to be entertained or be bored? Wouldn't you want the words and the visuals to be both stimulating and interesting? Would you want this production to be worth your time?

When developing movies, directors try to answer "yes" to these questions and try to exceed their audiences' expectations when they bring a film to screen. They read scripts and make movies out of them, whereas writers have ideas and transform them into scripts.

As the presenter, you are center stage, and it is up to you to try and meet the needs of your audience. You have to be both the writer and the director. In order to meet the needs of any audience, first examine who makes up the audience. Is the gender population mixed? What is the age group? Are there cultural differences?

The makeup of your audience is important to know. It is an essential part in preparing your material. The goal of any presentation is to have a purpose and to drive that purpose to the point of being received and understood. By gaining knowledge of your audience ahead of time, you can avoid unnecessary traps that can ruin your presentation.

Are They Intellectuals?

An intellectual, according to an Internet article, The Relationship Economy—Are Intellectuals Social? by Jay Deragon, is "a person who uses intelligence (thought and reason) and critical or analytical reasoning in either a professional or a personal capacity." They know many people but have very few people they talk to. They dislike gossip. They use their minds creatively and look for substance, not fluff. Beyond demanding it, they deliver it! Stick to the facts with intellects. They lose interest with a lot of repetition. Keep their attention by using examples; be lively but focused on your topic, and they will follow you to the last word you speak.

What Are Their Backgrounds?

How old are they? Find out as much information as possible about them. The goal is to make a dynamic first impression. The name of the game is to relate to your audience and meet them where they are. Don't blindly assume anything about your audience like their age, economic status, and social or emotional type. Find out as much information as you can.

What is the cultural makeup of your audience? It is so important to know the cultural composition of your audience. Do they speak and understand English or do you need a translator? Is there anything in the presentation that will offend a person because of cultural differences?

This is why doing your homework is crucial. South Miami Hospital's culture tool will help explain how important it is to relate to the people you are speaking to. If your audience or the person you are talking to is of Canadian descent, you should be aware that Canadians do not like a lot of touching. You should also avoid kissing them. They value honesty, and they take you at your word.

Now let's take a look at Cubans. Most Cubans, according to the culture tool, have a tendency to get loud when having a discussion and speak over one another. Cubans use their hands for emphasis and credibility, and they prefer strong eye contact.

You should know that the Indian Culture (Hindi) limits eye contact, and you should avoid touching him or her while talking.

Italians, on the other hand, are talkative, expressive, prefer eye to eye communication, and welcome personal and physical contact such as holding hands, patting on the back, and kissing.

Now with the Japanese, be aware that they avoid eye contact and touching. You should exercise caution while offering self-praise and acceptance of praise as each is considered inappropriate.

When in doubt about a particular culture, remain neutral. Be polite.

Watch how you are approached and watch the body language of the person. If the body language is friendly, this is usually an indicator that it is okay for you to react the same. If the person distances you, take the hint and give the person their space.

Many cultures are known to reject people touching them. But there is a "culture" that I have learned about that is called the touchy-feely people. Even when you tell them not to touch because it may or may not be politically accepted, they do it anyway. It is a natural response for them to touch or show love. They mean no harm. This is their way of connecting with another individual. Don't be surprised if you have a hand extended to shake and the person hugs you and in some instances gives you a kiss on the cheek. If you are a touchy-feely person, restrain yourself and read the body language or culture of your audience carefully.

What Are Their Spiritual Beliefs?

Determine the spiritual beliefs associated with your audience if, and only if, this information is something you need to know. Sometimes religion is obvious when a person is wearing religious garments or jewelry, and other times it is not. Take extreme caution to avoid offending or insulting someone if you are planning on using a religious example.

What Are Their Expectations?

The job of the presenter is to help get the audience on the same playing field. When delivering information that is heavy or very technical, try to simplify the material and make it enjoyable.

All audience members have an expectation. No one wants to sit and watch a movie or television program and feel they are wasting their time. The same is true for people listening to communication. They need to feel that it was planned, tailored to their needs, and has purpose.

Mark recently went to hear a person deliver a presentation on investing to improve finances. The presenter was briefly introduced by a very credible person with whom the audience was very familiar. There was one problem—the speaker went right into her presentation explaining how the rich people of Wall Street had caused our financial disaster in the twenty-first century. The audience was confused because the speaker worked for, and was a part of the same system as, the people she spoke about. The issue was the woman never introduced herself, nor did she qualify herself to the audience as an expert. She launched out and began her talk immediately after she was introduced. Every presenter must set his or her own stage and introduce themselves by presenting information that qualifies them to be an expert.

Mark was lost during the presentation and could not wait until it was over. This was because the introduction, which was vital to the rule of first impression, was not established and therefore led to obviously unplanned contradictions. Another distraction during this presentation was based on poor graphics. There were too many ideas on a page, and the information was too small to read. The talk could have hit a home run if the presenter had put more time into considering the audience's needs instead of playing the role of a hero by identifying and bashing her industry counterparts. Mark felt what took forty-five minutes to present could have been summed up in fifteen.

Key Points

- When looking at an audience, be conscious of their environment and why they are there. The presentation room or communication area may not be positive. If this is the case, try to make it as comfortable as possible for you and the audience. Sometimes an audience may even feel forced into an environment to listen to someone for a particular length of time. The act of being forced into a setting should be known upfront, so the presenter can gain an upper hand on the situation and reverse any negativity into time well spent with the speaker or speakers.

- Today, thanks to advancements in technology, your audience may be among millions in the cyberworld or on the Internet. You may or may not be able to attach a face to them. You may not know anything about this audience. It is up to you to create their profile and here is how one author goes about creating his characters. He mentally and physically creates the people in his books by drawing and making them stick figures and then he names them. Due to the unknown, your creation may consist of challenging and difficult people, like we discussed in Strategies 2 and 3, but still try to welcome them as well as embrace different cultures, genders, and ages into your presentation.

- Be aware of the time of day in which you are speaking. Not everyone is an early morning person. If the presentation is at 8 a.m. and your audience is made up of night people, the presenter must bring on some energy to keep the attention of the audience. The same applies if you are in the reverse situation and scheduled to speak at 4 p.m. You will have to rev it up and do what it takes to meet your audience's needs to gain and keep their attention. This should be considered and worked into the presentation.

- In preparing for your audience, always look at their purpose for being there. Do they want to be somewhat entertained, learn, or obtain solutions? The answer to all three is usually "yes."

An audience wants to feel that their presenter or communicator is knowledgeable, likable, and credible. Time is valuable. Fifteen minutes on a clock is still 900 seconds. The fifteen minutes can feel like an enjoyable five minutes, a tolerable fifteen minutes, or a bogged-down thirty minutes—boring! Again, we go back to watching a movie; your time is either well spent with the desire of wanting more, or the film is one that was a waste of time.

How to Handle the Disconnect

Connecting with your audience in any communication process is essential. Don't become misguided if you feel someone doesn't like or approve of you. Should you even care if they like you or not? To be liked is a natural desire. For people pleasers, it is a bigger expectation. If for some reason, you are not connecting with ten percent of the people around you, don't worry about it. Focus on the ninety percent who are responding positively.

Here are two tell-tale signs that indicate your audience is not engaged.

In diagram one, the woman has her back to the presenter texting, and in diagram two, the person is sleeping during a live webinar. Diagram three is an example of an engaged and attentive group.

Tips to Keep the Attention of Your Audience

- Engage your audience. Make them feel important and valued. Call people by their names and compliment when appropriate.

- Use friendly hand gestures and avoid pointing.

- Do not read to your audience. You may feel this is a given, but this rule is often violated, especially when using graphics.

- Respect the audience and summarize.

- Dress appropriately. Your clothing sends a message. If you want a positive first impression, dress for integrity.

- Be conversational. Your tone can make or break your ability to keep an audience's attention. Reread **Strategy 4** for ways to improve your voice. Work to perfect your craft. It is a valuable resource.

- Be organized. Structure your material into the order you desire. Make sure the order builds logically and is easy to digest; then practice, practice, practice!

- Take your audience on a smooth journey. The more you are familiar with your organized work, the better your presentation will flow.

- Be interesting. This can be challenging, but find relevant stories and examples to weave into your presentation.

- Know your stuff. Research your subject matter. It is insulting to an audience to listen to someone who is not knowledgeable or prepared.

- Allow interaction. If appropriate, let the audience participate or be involved somehow throughout the program (questions, skits, role-play, etc.). Structure group time to role-play or to examine a case study. Be creative to break up a lecture-style setup.

- Use technology wisely and creatively. Practice with it. If technology adds worth to your delivery, use it. If it doesn't add clarity, avoid it.

- Respect your audience, put yourself in their shoes. Give the same respect you want to receive. Try to make your time together a pleasant one for all.

Challenge

This is your production! What attributes do you possess that can be integrated into your presentation or conversation to help you connect with your audience?

Declaration

I connect well with my audience. They understand the material I am delivering, and they love to hear me speak. I add value to my audience.

- Strategy 8 -

ENGAGE YOUR AUDIENCE

> **And he said unto them, "He that hath ears to hear, let him hear."**
> **Mark 4:9, King James Version**

Prepare Your Ears to Hear! Have you ever listened to a television or radio interview, and you just wanted to tell the host to let the interviewee tell their story without interrupting them? When interviewing, the job of the host is to keep the interview flowing. This is not a time for the host to make the show about him or her.

I interviewed a profound expert in the field of finance named Catrice Wells. She is the author of When Heaven Went Public. During the television interview, I probably talked less than any other interview I've conducted. After setting the flow of the interview, I noticed that Catrice was in a rhythm, so I let her explain to the audience how they could help improve their financial outlook. I didn't interrupt because she was getting more talk time than me. The audience was engaged, and an unnecessary interruption could have led to lost pertinent information.

A good interview host knows when to talk and when to listen. That's a lesson for us all. James 1:19 tells us, "Let every man be swift to hear, slow to speak." In our daily conversations, we should know when to listen and when to speak.

Here's an exercise for you. Close your eyes and just listen. I am purposely writing this section of this book outside on my patio. I hear birds chirping, lawn mowers eating up grass, planes flying, leaves being blown by the wind, cars passing, and various other unidentifiable noises. With my eyes closed, the sounds come together like a symphonic concert. I can hear all the parts of the orchestra.

When I open my eyes, it is harder for me to focus on the symphony. The visual element adds a distraction as I see a bird flying by. I am now more focused on the sounds of the chirping and singing of the birds. The other atmospheric sounds fade into a less noticeable state. A plane just flew by with a banner attached to it. It was low and very loud. This sound overrode all the other sounds. I was completely focused on it as it passed.

This exercise hopefully shows you that your attention will be focused on whatever your vision and mind will permit. Unless you refocus your attention, the distractions will take over and rule your day. That is what this strategy is all about.

Epictetus, a Greek stoic philosopher, is attributed to the phrase, "We have two ears and one mouth so that we can listen twice as much as we speak." But do we use our two ears to listen twice as much? Not everyone knows how to be good and effective listeners. To be a good listener, you have to be patient, considerate, and comfortable in your own skin.

John is cocky and loves to talk. He is the president of his own fan club. He even has a chant to let you know. It goes like this: "I'm John Brown, president of my own fan club. I'm wonderful and everyone knows it." John hardly ever listens to people speak. He rudely interrupts speakers to get his point across. He is a master at rushing a conversation and steering it into his control or direction. John, for some reason, has to be the center of every conversation. He is a good example of a person who is not patient, confident, considerate, or comfortable in his own skin.

Becky, on the other hand, is patient and will listen to a person communicate for a great length of time. She enjoys experiencing life through the stories of others, listening and then adding feedback when it is necessary. She is not into one-up activities, controlling conversations, or speaking just to hear herself talk.

To become an effective listener, you must make a choice; it's simple to listen or not to. It takes three seconds to consciously shift gears and decide to listen to a person. For example, you must actively say to yourself, Bill wants to tell me something, so I'm going to listen. Listening is vital in every form of communication. It is not a passive activity; it is an active choice.

Five Hindrances to Listening

•Sleepiness–the person may be too tired to listen.

•Boredom–the person may not be interested in the subject matter.

•Disability/mental stress–the person for physical or mental reasons cannot maintain focus.

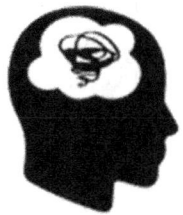

- Disconnection–the person does not like or agree with the speaker or subject matter.

- Wandering mind–the person desires to be somewhere else.

Research reveals that the average attention span of an adult is twenty-two seconds, and that adults only retain twenty-five percent of what they hear. This, of course, pertains to individuals who are not taught to listen. These statistics are really sad but are understandable when you consider the hindrances.

People generally pay attention to whoever talks louder. Our attention may be directed to the person, but there is a question as to whether or not we comprehend what is going on. People who shout often feel they can control conversations by yelling. Our hearing devices may hear them, but our brains may decide to ignore their words.

People generally pay attention to whoever talks louder.

Listening takes patience. In our world today, we live in a fast-paced society where the goal is to get whatever we want or need as quickly as possible. If we have to wait at a drive-through for five minutes, some of us become unnerved and complain about the poor service. There is another way of looking at the situation, such as the food is being prepared safely and with some care as opposed to being microwaved and thrown together.

Not only is it important to exercise patience when listening, it is equally necessary to discipline yourself for listening. It can be extremely difficult for people to listen to someone speak, communicate in the process, and take notes. For years, I trained consultants from various parts of the country, who had difficulty balancing and juggling this act of communicating and taking notes. First of all, this particular group of individuals seemed intimidating to their audience. So any time they picked up a pen or started typing in their laptops, it was determined that they must be writing something bad about the person or their organization.

To avoid this feeling, I advised consultants to inform staff that they would take notes to jog their memory about good things that they observed and what they needed to follow up on. To further ease tension, the consultants were instructed to give as much eye contact as possible and nod to let staff know they were listening.

When people feel they are not being heard, they have a tendency to shut down communication. So many times, individuals are rushed in their current analysis of a staff presentation in order to make it to the next staff presentation. They become challenged to listen to answers they are receiving while mentally planning for their next location and round of questions.

The best way to stay focused on the matter at hand is to actively use your voice as a remote control. Click it and say, "I am going to listen to Bradley because he has something he wants to tell me." When Bradley pauses, this is your cue to take control of the conversation. People know when no one is listening to them. One big indication is when someone is talking at the same time as you. The words listen and silent are made from the same letters. There's a reason for this.

Counselors are usually known to be patient and great listeners. I know this one particular psychologist who sits and listens to at least a hundred situations from different people every week. You would never know it. He treats everyone as if their story or dilemma is as important to him as it is to them. His listening skills and patience are gifts from God.

Good listeners are generally people who can help resolve conflicts, build trust, inspire people, strengthen teams, and find solutions to problems. The key is that they respect people enough to value them and hear what they are saying and not saying. They are able to put their own personal issues aside and listen to what is spoken or not spoken through body language. Poor listening habits will guarantee loss of information and failure for others to interact and respond appropriately.

Good listeners are generally people who can help resolve conflicts, build trust, inspire people, strengthen teams, and find solutions to problems.

We not only listen to our words and the words of others, but we also listen nonverbally. Our minds, bodies, and spirits speak to us. The question is whether we listen. Remember Ginger? She said she had always battled negative thoughts in her mind, telling her that she was an ineffective communicator and that she didn't measure up to other people. Ginger responded by shutting down and walking with slumped posture. She needed to focus on the words of Paul, found in Philippians 4:8 "Think on things that are true, honest, just, pure, lovely, and of good report." She had spent many years believing a lie. No matter what others thought about her positively, she felt the opposite because a voice inside of her was telling her that people were lying. Ginger had to make the decision to ignore the voice and speak the Word of God, saying that she is fearfully and wonderfully made.

Can we listen to our bodies? An ache, pain, or discomfort says to us that it wants our attention, and we normally will respond. My son had severe asthma as a child. It was not unusual for him to tell my husband and me that it was time to go to the hospital. I would always ask him if he was sure, and he would say, "Yes, let's go." Sure enough, every time, he was placed in intensive care.

I interviewed a person who had lost his leg in an accident. He was hospitalized for months and nearly died. He was determined after much therapy to live his life to the fullest. He didn't listen to the limitations that were presented. He decided to master his new body, and today he is a competitive athlete running, swimming, and biking. He is working and doing everything he did before the accident. He refused to listen to his body and the threats of limitations that said, "Your life is over!"

In a conversation with a struggling high school student, I merely asked her if she could envision herself graduating. She told me that she couldn't see it happening. She would have been the first in her family to graduate. The voices in her head told her that she wouldn't, and guess what? She didn't! If only she hadn't listened.

How Do You Know When Someone Is Listening?

Direct eye contact, head nods, and leaning forward to listen are usually true signs to let a person know they are being heard. The word hear is mentioned in the Bible 550 times. When God spoke, just as when we speak, He expected people to listen, including Adam and Eve who disobeyed him in the Garden of Eden. But how do you really know if someone hears you or even understands you? That question is raised more and more when we examine writings in print and social media. Messages written via emails, texting, Facebook, and Twitter, can't be read, deciphered, or understood with a head nod, direct eye contact, or any other body language. The tone is determined and interpreted by the reader, and what is understood may very well be completely different from what the originator of the material meant.

Emoji art is a digital language added to the unspoken word to produce clarity. The icons or images usually express an idea or emotion. Emojis can be used to bridge the gap between the mind and the heart. This electronic communication also allows some individuals to add content beyond what they can express in writing. Emoji messages are usually quickly and easily interpreted and understood. A picture is said to be worth a thousand words.

In like manner, hashtags are another form of nonverbal communication that is gathering momentum with social media. Much can be learned from these little phrases. They capture the most important words without writing a full sentence, making it easier to rapidly scan, find events, and respond. Emojis are much easier to universally recognize, read, and communicate than the hashtags that are being used today.

As mentioned in the introduction of this book, we communicate in three different ways: with our words, our body language, and our spirit. The same applies to listening. A person who can't physically hear with their ears will indicate how they can feel and interpret what a person is communicating to them. Even though the sounds may not be recognized by them physically, they can feel the person's spirit and interpret a person's body language and determine whether it is friendly or hostile.

Listening is a gift. When one listens, it opens the door to understanding and direction. Everyone wants to be heard and validated. Listening also sets a foundation for building positive relationships.

Build Relationships

God has planted a desire in all of us to have positive relationships. "The Lord God said, 'It is not good for the man to be alone'" (Genesis 2:18, New International Version). Whether the relationship is with family or friends, deep down inside, we all want those relationships to be healthy. The problem is, do we want to take the time and effort to make them healthy?

There are benefits to having healthy relationship:

>1. **You will feel good about yourself.** Being in a favorable relationship means that you have someone who believes in you and validates you. This validation is vital. We all feel good when someone we trust tells us they feel our pain, and they love and care for us no matter what not by words alone, but by action.

>2. **You will have less stress.** In life, we are tested on so many levels. To internalize and bear all the burdens yourself is insane. A good friend can offer sound counsel and comfort even if that means shedding tears together or offering alternatives for the moment. Stress can be relieved by having a prayer partner or friend to pray with you, validate your pain, or just hold your hand.

>3. **You feel happier.** God didn't design us to be alone. Proverbs 18:1 NKJV says, "Whoever isolates himself seeks his own desire." Ecclesiastes 4:10 NIV-MIT reads, "If one falls down, his friend can help him up, but pity the man who falls and has no one to help him."

>4. **You feel safe around the person or persons.** When the spirit of one person connects with the spirit of another and both of you find comfort, this is what I am referring to as feeling safe. I was on vacation in Florida and met a woman at the resort I was staying. We both knew instantly that it was a divine appointment because our spirits connected. After talking briefly, I realized that God had

placed her in my life to give me direction about something with which I was struggling. She realized she was the connector. We both knew our meeting had purpose and that it wasn't an accident. Have you ever visited a person with Alzheimer's you've previously had a relationship with, but they have forgotten your name? I have a friend I went to visit, and she grabbed me and told me how a close relative of hers had died. She was so happy to see me and gave me great detail of her feelings about her loss. My friend couldn't give any background information about our relationship, nor remember my name, but in the spirit world, we connected. She knew I was a safe person. You will know in your spirit when you feel safe with someone or not; there is either peace or a message of warning.

5. **You can trust your secrets to the other person(s)**. Many of us don't want to talk about our problems because we don't feel safe and secure with the thought that someone will expose our business and even our pain. When you find someone who has your back and you can trust, it is a good thing. God says we can always cast our burdens on Him, and we should. Because He desires for us to not be alone, He also sends a good person into our lives with whom we can feel safe enough to share details.

Spend Time

Spending time with people is how you build relationships. I have been blessed to have a friendship with someone special since first grade. Her name is Jackie. She and I are alike in many ways but also different. For instance, both of us love to decorate. We share that hobby. Her decorating style is more French provincial, and mine is described as contemporary. Both of us love elegance. We are both very independent. We both share thoughts and secrets about each other, although we don't always agree. We never have a problem telling each other when we think the other is wrong. We both work hard, but she gets out and travels and enjoys life more. In this area, I am more like Martha in the Bible, and she is more like Mary.

We both have gone through some pretty hard times. One of those occurred when her mother and my father were both hospitalized in the same hospital at the same time, and ironically on the same floor. Her mother had been diagnosed with cancer and had been dealing with it for a couple of years. My father, who had hardly even been sick, had a stroke. I called Jackie to tell her that I thought she should fly in to be with her mother after she was admitted to the hospital. Jackie had just taken her mom on a vacation to Niagara Falls and had just left her but came back to Illinois, and both of us spent time with each other and our parents in the hospital. Both of our parents died within a week of one another. Again, the two little girls who climbed trees and sat there for hours to hide away from monstrous issues were together again as if no time had passed. We helped each other out during the difficult transition of our last living parents.

Relationships grow when you spend time with each other. You don't have to talk every day because all it takes is a bond between you and the other person. There will automatically be a desire to share information if trust and respect are present.

Jackie and I don't see each other much because she lives in North Carolina, and I live in Illinois. We talk on our birthdays, in December (the month we lost our parents), and maybe two or three times during the year. Even though we don't talk often, I know that she's got my back, and I have hers. If I am hurting, I know who to call, and the same goes for her. We don't judge each other. We confront issues and get raw with one another whether the other person wants to hear it or not. In the end, she knows I'm right, and in the end, I know she is right. We then appropriately line up our lives. For some reason, Jackie feels like she is the older, protective one of the two of us. We are the same age. I am two months older, but you would think she was ten years older. She never had a sister, so I guess I am the person who fills the younger sister role she so desires in her life. I am the oldest of five children and don't have an older sister or brother, so this relationship works for me as well.

Respect People

My former trainer often told me he only spent time with people who celebrate him and not those who tolerate him. He doesn't try to force himself on anyone. People who respect you will care about you. The Bible says in Luke 6:31, "And as ye would that men should do to you, do ye also to them likewise." In other words, "do unto others as you would have them do unto you".

Respect is important in a relationship, and it means different things to many people. The late Jackie Robinson, the first black baseball player in the major leagues, said, "I'm not concerned with your liking or disliking me...all I ask is that you respect me as a human being."

To Gloria, a wife of nearly forty years, respect may look like her husband opening the car door for her or her husband walking with her instead of an eighth of a mile ahead of her. Carl may internalize disrespect as his wife hollers and blames him for his shortcomings. It may also be in the form of a spouse blaming the other for financial problems while one of them has a secret stash on the side to enjoy. Disrespect also occurs when a person intentionally blocks someone in a parking garage and purposefully prevents them from exiting. The thing to remember is, it is not about you. The other person may have an issue with control and superiority. Don't get caught up in their web and remember that life is not all about them. Respect yourself and demand it from others.

> **According to the late Maya Angelou, "If we lose love and self-respect for each other, this is how we finally die."**

What does self-respect look and feel like? Self-respect says: I love and care about me. I appreciate who I am. No one with a negative tongue can define me. I do not set out to purposefully destroy my body. I have purpose and want to bless the world with who God made me. When I respect myself, I am more apt to respect others.

When one respects him or herself, there are automatic rules that manifest: (1)They don't harm themselves, (2)they value who they are,(3)they take time to celebrate themselves, and most importantly, (4) they don't give their power over to people who set out to purposely hurt them. People who disrespect others are people who usually lack self-respect for themselves. They should not be allowed to spew their poison on whomever whenever they please.

Jessie and Carlos think they have a great friendship. Jessie is the one always taking care of Carlos when he is in financial and emotional need. Jessie, unfortunately, went through a heartbreaking experience, which ended up causing him to make some extremely poor decisions in his life. Instead of Carlos being supportive, he took the opportunity to blame Jessie for putting himself in that position which he personally knew was not true. Jessie even witnessed an occasion when Carlos was whispering and pointing to another person about him. This is one of many times Carlos spoke against his friend. Jessie immediately saw his friend in a new light, as a person who lacked integrity and who could not stand up and acknowledge wrongdoing. Carlos condemned him. However, Jessie wisely created space between them.

Why? Jessie had too much respect for himself to be subjected to Carlos' character assassination.

The People Society Respects

Let's examine the people many say they admire and respect. Oprah Winfrey is a name that is often mentioned as are Senator Ted Kennedy, Jacqueline Onassis, Barbara Walters, Steve Jobs, Bill Gates, Denzel Washington, Presidents Roosevelt, Kennedy, Reagan, Clinton, and Obama. The list goes on and on. All of these people have shown a rare form of self-respect.

What do they all have in common? They possess an obvious respect for themselves as well as others. They all have gained respect in their various jobs or professions. They are and were influential and have all made major contributions to our world. So, if a person's goal is to be respected, what must happen?

1. Internalize the goal.

2. Know that you are worthy of respect and have an expectancy to receive it.

3. Act with integrity.

4. Act as if you are proud of who you are and have a character that reflects honesty and trust worthiness.

5. Give of yourself. Your experiences, knowledge, and abilities are all qualities you possess. They are valuable. Be a resource to others.

6. Accept respect. Say to yourself, "I respect myself and others, and they too respect me." Own respect and walk into your arena. Ignore voices inside your head feeding doubts and contradicting who you are in God's eyes. Psalm 139:14 says that you are "fearfully and wonderfully made."

I like this quote from author Stephen Covey. He says, "Trust is the glue of life. It's the most essential ingredient in effective communication. It's the foundational principle that holds all relationships." Without trust, there is always going to be something missing. It is crucial for building positive relationships.

Ways to Build Positive Relationships While Communicating

Use your words carefully. Words are vehicles for communication, and communication drives the messages. The messages are interpreted based on the understanding of the communicators.

For example, Will was delivering a presentation and in a joking manner said, "You all are crazy." He was speaking to mental health professionals. They were immediately offended. Among each other, they have made jokes that they had to be insane to do what they do, but for an outsider to come in and make that statement was unacceptable.

Words can hurt. You've heard the saying, "Sticks and stones can break my bones, but words can never hurt me." This is a lie!

Gina worked for a hospice organization and would often say to family of deceased individuals, "I know how you feel." Of course, the obvious response in one's thoughts are, You don't know exactly how I feel.

A better way of handling both Will's and Gina's situations would be to take a more individualized approach. In Will's case, he could have said, "I can appreciate what you're saying," instead of using words that pointed a finger at the group. In the situation with Gina, a better approach might have been to say, "I can understand how you'd feel that way." Again, we can empathize with others, but if you haven't shared the same experience or don't have the same background as others, it is better to play it safe and talk from your perspective.

The goal in using the more than 171,000 words contained in the dictionary is to choose them and use them effectively to build relationships. Here are some tips to help: Always remember to introduce yourself when talking to someone new, be pleasant and polite, and state your purpose for the conversation. People are more apt to talk to you when they know who you are and your purpose for communicating with them.

Create an impression in your mind of how you will build any relationship. If you see yourself winning in the first ninety seconds, your body language will follow. On the other hand, if you show dislike and shoot negative darts within this time frame, I guarantee your conversation will not be effective. Studies show that people are more motivated to participate when they are treated with respect. Research also reveals that people who receive compliments create an atmosphere of cooperation when communicating. Another way to build relationships is to smile. It's been said that people who smile appear to be more confident and are easier to approach. A smile can go a long way to ease intimidation and set a tone of friendliness when communicating.

Make sure gestures and nonverbal cues match verbal communication. Here is an all-too-familiar example. Sue opened a gift from Bob and said, "I really like the gift." The words came out of her mouth, but her body language told an entirely different story as she held the bold yellow tablecloth-type dress away from her body. The nonverbal will always tell the real story because actions speak louder than words.

Be conversational. Newspapers are written at approximately an eighth-grade reading level. The press releases received from the White House are said to be written at this same level. Proving yourself to be smarter by using b-i-g words does not help to build relationships. Relax and be conversational. There is a time and purpose to exhibit one's vocabulary. If the purpose is to be superior, it could harm the relationship you are trying to build.

- Use good quality of voice. Avoid being boisterous.
- Use friendly tones.
- Use repetition creatively. If you need to ask someone to repeat something, you can simply say, "Please give me an example." It in turn tells the person you are talking to that you just asked a different question.
- Use good eye contact. Negative results are produced when people are not looking at the person or the audience in general. If this is hard for you to do, as I mentioned before, please focus your attention on the upper bridge of one's nose between their two eyes. When there isn't eye contact, a third person called low self-esteem enters the conversation, and it becomes the main topic.

Technology and the Relationship

The Evans family are all home by 6 p.m. The older son is playing video games with his friends in the family room. The two daughters are in their rooms texting friends. Mom's cooking dinner and calls all the children on their cell phones to let them know dinner is ready. Meanwhile, dad is on the computer playing games in the man cave to wind down. Where is the face-to-face communication?

We are losing a war on relationships if we don't manage our texts, tweets, Facebook conversations, and other social media options. I find that more and more teenagers are verbally communicating less, and it is becoming acceptable. Children are even coming to dinner tables with their cell phones. Instead of communicating with one another during this time, many are reacting to the emails or texts they receive. The misuse of technology can rob us of getting to know one another. Technology has a purpose and a place and so does verbal communication. God didn't tweet the world into existence; He spoke it.

God didn't tweet the world into existence; He spoke it.

Create Intimacy in the Relationship with Your Audience

What is intimacy in a relationship? It generally refers to being in a close personal association and belonging together. It is a familiar and very close effective connection with another as a result of a bond that is formed through knowledge and experience of the other. Genuine intimacy in human relationships requires honesty.

Intimacy is a gift. It is the ultimate giving of one's heart. I believe it is what God intended for Adam and Eve. It is so much more than sex. It's the sharing of spirit, mind, body, and soul, on a unique level so few get to experience. I have seen it in several couples, particularly in older ones. My former pastor, Dr. Isaac Singleton, told his wife every day of their lives together that he loved her. That is the one thing she said she missed the most since he passed away. They had been married for sixty-five years.

Inviting someone into your world to experience "you" can be very frightening. We are cautious individuals.

I love what Marshall Hodge wrote about intimacy in his book called *Your Fear of Love,* "We long for moments of expressions of love, closeness and tenderness, but frequently, at the critical point, we often draw back. We are afraid of closeness. We are afraid of love. The closer you come to somebody, the greater potential there is for pain. It is the fear of pain that often drives us away from finding true intimacy."

Believe it or not, this pain can lead people to create stop signs and even purposely sabotage relationships. This is another example of how people try hard to stay where they are. This type of communicator won't allow themselves to enjoy life or their family to full potential. They often times feel people are against them. They blame others when things go wrong. Deep down, they feel they don't deserve happiness. They can be mean and cruel. Many times something happened that sabotaged their belief system to make them reject closeness and any resemblance of oneness. Some have never seen intimacy. Advice most psychologists offer is to love them as long as they are not being abusive.

Saboteurs in the business world have put up fences to keep you out. As the relationship builds to a point of letting you into their area, don't be surprised if they find some type of fault in you. This action is supposed to prompt you to give them the space they are used to possessing. If a person who desires to be closer tries to go beyond this invisible mark, the relationship could end. It takes a caring and nurturing person to break through layers of pain and hurt to show love and trust to the saboteur. This can be done by working slowly with the saboteur and backing off when you feel the rejection. Eventually, the saboteur (if he or she desires) will learn to trust you and allow you to see their heart. One point of advice: Avoid using the word *you*. It sends daggers through a saboteur's heart, and it also tells them to close the door because you are trying to hurt or punish them. Tread lightly, for this person has to grow in love. Compliment them often.

Create a Positive Relationship with Your Audience

Acknowledge them. Design the audience into your presentation. An audience can be used in two ways: as a sounding board or an intricate part of your presentation to bring it alive and make it more meaningful. Gesture toward them without pointing. Move away from a podium environment and mingle closer to their seated area. This does not mean walking into the audience and up to the people in rows 3, 5, or 9, violating comfort zones.

Create involvement. Encourage feedback at some point in your presentation. This can be done with interaction during or after your presentation. Also, welcome questions. Always remember you are the authority on your subject matter. Questions help to clarify information, to retain information, and to set up dialogue with the audience.

Engage your Audience with appropriate eye contact. Staring at the back wall while delivering information is a complete turn off. By using appropriate eye contact, focusing on a few people on the left side of the room, then shifting to the right smoothly, and coming back to the center creates a connection between the audience and the speaker. Combine this with mentioning a few names during the presentation, which tells your audience they are important enough for you to involve them.

Allowing your audience to ask questions and asking questions yourself are both great ways to keep your audience engaged. Choose the best time to entertain questions. Options include an open forum where questions can be asked randomly to make a more interactive presentation or welcome them only at the end of your presentation. This is your choice. Another way for questions to be used is by raising them yourself during your presentation. These questions are designed for nonverbal feedback such as, "How many of you would love to make money while you sleep?" "Are you tired of our old, prehistoric phone system? How many of you would like this new innovative process to make your life easier and provide you with extra income?"

You, the presenter, can even raise your hand; this gesture shows the audience how to respond. These questions are designed to shift the conversation to sell your idea, product, or thought process. This process is called "anchoring and tie backs." You now have engaged your audience; use this opportunity to drive and sell your point.

Silence the Voices in Your Head

The enemy's mission as mentioned earlier is to steal, kill, and destroy. Know who your enemy is. His purpose is to keep you from developing strong relationships and succeeding. If he can isolate you and keep you open to his negative dialogue of lies, he's won half the battle in destroying you.

Instead of listening to voices telling you that you are unattractive, unsuccessful, you don't stack up, everyone hates being around you, people don't like talking or listening to you, or you are weird, uneducated, too fat or too skinny and so forth, commit to stop the madness. Stop going around the same mountain and envision yourself winning the battle.

It's simple; find a Scripture stating who you are in Christ and tell the devil that he is a liar. Examples:

- **Philippians 4:13**—"I can do all things through Christ who strengthens me."

- **Deuteronomy 28:13**—"And the Lord will make you the head and not the tail; you shall be above only, and not be beneath, if you heed the commandments of the Lord your God, which I command you today, and are careful to observe them."

- **2 Timothy 1:7, New King James Version**—"For God has not given us a spirit of fear, but of power and of love and of a sound mind."

Create a new image of yourself by saying, "I am happy and not sad, I am enjoyable to be around, I am beautiful/handsome, and I am strong and not weak." Let's not forget Ginger who doesn't like to be around others and thinks people feel the same about her. She convinced herself that she is unacceptable and doesn't fit in. She also thinks she's unattractive. She is very uncomfortable and full of anxiety when she's around a group of people.

This is the report that the enemy painted of Ginger. The truth is, Ginger is very attractive, highly intelligent, a master of the English language, and is enjoyable to be around. Ginger, unfortunately, does not recognize this version of the herself.

Because of this negative profile, Ginger has battled anxiety, depression, and self-worth issues for most of her life. When Ginger decided to fight back, regain her life, and build relationships with meaningful people, she began to confess who she was according to her Creator.

Her dialogue of positive self-affirming words changed her life. She now believes something new and exciting. "People love to listen to me talk. I love to listen to them. I accept and love me."

When Ginger's self-talk changed about herself, her life changed. Relationships (whether in front of an audience or her personal ones) blossomed.

Challenge

What personal traits do you possess to foster positive relationships? What negative self-talk are you entertaining? Choose to be an active listener.

Declaration

I choose to be engaged with my audience. I have a positive image. I choose to be a good listener and welcome intimacy into my relationships. I own my stage.

Part III

Enjoy Your Stage

- Strategy 9 -

ENJOY YOURSELF

> Charge them that are rich in this world, that they be not high minded, nor trust in uncertain riches, but in the living God, who giveth us richly all things to enjoy.
> I Timothy 6:17, King James Version

You can enjoy the process! God wants to richly bless our lives It is His desire for us to enjoy life. Usually when I stand before a group of people and ask them to acknowledge whether or not they enjoy speaking in front of others, only twenty percent of the people holdup their hands. This number increases, of course, after they have received formal training. The good news is everyone can communicate and enjoy the process.

Enjoyment Is Contagious

A night out with true friends can really be an enjoyable time. Picture this scene: good food, a relaxed atmosphere, laughter in the air, plenty of dancing, and the comedians of the group talking their A-game. Some doctors believe this is a prescription in itself.

Stress, according to the American Medical Association, is a factor in more than seventy-five percent of today's sicknesses. According to the World Health Organization, stress is America's number one health problem. In a poll conducted in 2004 by the American Psychological Association, seventy-three percent of Americans name money as the culprit for their stress while sixty-two percent say their work has a significant impact on their stress levels. With the economy slowly recovering after the recession of 2008, one can imagine that the stress levels are much higher now with companies downsizing and people losing their jobs and homes.

So, letting our hair down and having a good time can be very healthy. We have been designed by God to enjoy life. In 1 Peter 5:7, (New International Version) we're told, "Cast all your anxiety on him because he cares for you." Philippians 4:19 also assures us that God will supply all our needs. We are to accept God's gift of enjoyment according to the encouragement found in 1 Timothy 6:17.

According to a 2006 study conducted by Sophie Scott, a neuroscientist at the University College London, "Laughter truly is contagious: the brain responds to the sound of laughter and preps the muscles in the face to join in the mirth."

"It seems that it's absolutely true that 'laugh and the whole world laughs with you.' We've known for some time that when we are talking to someone, we often mirror their behavior, copying the words they use and mimicking their gestures. Now we've shown that the same appears to apply to laughter, too, at least at the level of the brain."

Just as laughter is contagious, anything we enjoy can be contagious—even speaking to our audience. The dictionary defines contagious as "tending to spread from person to person: contagious laughter." Ralph Waldo Emerson says, "Vigor is contagious, and whatever makes us either think or feel strongly adds to our power and enlarges our field of action."

Can you think of some speakers or entertainers who spark a contagious interest and/or enjoyment in their audiences? Let's look at some of the highly-rated television shows. For nearly three decades, millions have loved the Oprah Winfrey Show. They have been drawn to her because many feel she is genuine, giving, and relatable. Television shows such as The Dick Van Dyke Show, I Love Lucy, Star Trek, Scandal, and soap operas still keep millions watching for pleasure. Oh, and I must include The Nanny because it was a show I watched before bed. It actually calmed me, and I laughed royally. It was my way of relieving the stress of the day.

People are and have been drawn to great speakers in the political world as well, such as U.S. Presidents Reagan, Clinton, and Obama. These presidents as well as others have attracted large numbers of supporters.

As communicators, we all have the same ability to draw our audiences to a place of enjoyment. First believe people want to listen to you. Second, confess that the audience will love what you have to say, and third, you must enjoy the process. Then you will see and feel the joy rub off on your audience. They will catch your spirit.

> **As communicators, we all have the same ability to draw our audiences to a place of enjoyment. Start by believing people want to listen to you.**

You're Center Stage

As a communicator, you control your arena. It is yours to enjoy. Speakers who are most relaxed and comfortable while speaking are those who have something thoughtful to say. Those who have not done the proper prep or research are less comfortable in front of others. Let's look at some scenarios where the outcomes are different based on prep, research, and inner joy.

Scenario 1

Version A
A fire broke out in the 1600 block of Canton. The entire cul-de-sac was blocked off. Local reporters were dispatched to the scene. Reporter

Tony Smith stated, "About three hundred firemen are on the scene of this fire. No one seems to know why or how it got started. Officials say arson may have been to blame. At this time, reports indicate there may be injuries, but we do not have confirmation on that yet. At least twenty people may be injured. We will have more details about the victims of this fire from our correspondents at surrounding hospitals. The one thing we can tell you is the fire is near containment. Winds have died down, and the firefighters, according to the chief, say the worst is over. We will now go to Marlene Dozer, at Canton Memorial Hospital, for an update on the conditions of victims there. Marlene?"

Version B
As we change over to Channel 6's local reporter, Edward Cane, this is the report, "We just received word that some thirty people have died as result of a fire located in the 1600 block of Canton. Chief Baker is with me. Chief, can you tell us how this fire started, was it from an electrical situation, is that how these people lost their lives?"

Chief Baker then states, "I don't know where you got your information, but we do not know the cause of this fire, and we have not mentioned anything about fatalities or injuries. Our investigation is still in progress. You should check your facts before you announce and spark fear in your viewers." Edward was speechless, paused with his microphone, and then said, "Back to you in the studio."

Scenario 2

Version A
James spent weeks preparing for a speech to be delivered to senior management at his company. He studied and researched all the information on the topic thoroughly. After writing his speech and adding creativity to it, he practiced it. Senior management loved the presentation. They loved it so much that he was promoted.

Version B

Jack was given the same opportunity to address senior staff. He too researched material and put his speech together but did so overnight and presented it the next day. Senior management was disappointed because he read his presentation and lacked key elements to prove his point, which ultimately led staff to not buy in to his proposal.

Scenario 3

Version A

It's Sunday morning, and the church is full. The choir was awesome and the congregation is expecting a hallelujah message. Reverend Brown comes to the microphone and says, "Praise God! We are going to do something different today. My wife and I just got back from vacation, and I just want to tell you all about the wonderful time we had. We really relaxed. All of you should relax like that sometime. We ate and ate and drank all the Shirley Temples we wanted. (I know many of you thought I was going to say we drank something else!) We loved the ocean. I even went snorkeling. God is good!" The congregation shouts back, "Amen!" "Well," he says, "That's all I have for you today, let's open the doors of the church and go home." Parishioners looked at each other in amazed disappointment.

Version B

That same Sunday morning at another church, Pastor Triplet was flowing in the spirit. Some of the best gospel music was sung. People were shouting. Pastor Triplett got up and said, "I am going to talk about what to do when you don't know what to do." He talked about being placed in situations when you'd rather disappear. He gave several Scripture references showing how God is always there, and no matter what situation you're in, He can deliver you. He reminded the people to always remember that all things are possible with God. After church, many people proclaimed to one another that Pastor Triplet really preached. One woman commented, "He must have known what I've been going through."

Prep Matters

Obviously, these are two versions of the same situations but what makes them different? What is apparent in all of these scenarios? Prep or the lack thereof. The reporters at the Canton fire both visually saw the same fire. Their stories were different as were their facts. Tony is an award-winning reporter because he digs deep and goes beyond the norm when investigating. He is very passionate about his job and wants to report the news as accurately as possible. Edward, on the other hand, doesn't share or value this same sense of excellence. Later, the station manager asked Edward to reveal his source for the story, and he replied, "An onlooker." Instead of checking with the station, Edward just took the word of someone on the street. He didn't go the extra mile to double-check his sources and facts.

In scenarios three and four, our presenters were surprised to learn that the senior management of a firm was looking to promote someone to a director's position. They had their eyes on two individuals, James and Jack. Without letting them know, management decided they were going to base their decision on the outcome of a proposal. James put a lot of work into preparing, but Jack didn't. James' hard work paid off and earned him a promotion. It appears that Jack ineffectively prepared his presentation.

In looking at our two preachers, it seemed obvious that Reverend Brown enjoyed his vacation and did not prepare a sermon for that particular Sunday. Pastor Triplett, on the other hand, planned a most memorable message.

Prep can mean the difference between being successful or less than average. We can all tell if we are stimulating our audience in a positive way. A polished presentation comes from research and great prep. You know when it is there and when it is lacking. Stumbling, repeating unnecessarily, omitting pertinent information, or simply wasting people's time may be the result if there is minimal preparation. One fact is certain; the speaker who is unprepared is not enjoying the process of communicating. Instead of flowing in ease, usually there are significant signs of internal struggling.

So when we fail to prep, what is the result? We fail to change lives, motivate people, get that job we say we want, or educate our audiences to the fullest degree. To learn more about prepping for a presentation, reread **Strategy 5, Prepare Your Material.**

Next, let's look at some other obstacles that hinder us from enjoying the process.

Hindrances of Joy

Thoughts: Our thinking determines what quality of life we experience. "A good man out of the good treasure of his heart brings forth good; and an evil man out of the evil treasure of his heart brings forth evil" (Luke 6:45, NKJV). Own your destiny and be willing to work on yourself by doing whatever it takes to reinvent yourself and give birth to a greater you.

Remember, the "Get a Mac" campaigns that were designed to showcase the weaknesses of the PC and the superior effectiveness of the MAC? In Apple's award-winning commercial, the PC representative was made to feel as if he did not measure up to the standards and acceptance of the competitor. The MAC representative, however, was confident and on top of his game. In life, many people take on the role and the perceived identity of the PC and box themselves into a life with limits.

Life is to be enjoyed. Some people don't allow themselves to enjoy it because they feel like the PC in the ad campaigns. They have something to prove, and they think they don't quite measure up. In general, people usually evaluate the quality of life by looking at the good versus the bad and comparing. Theodore Roosevelt once wisely said, "Comparison is the thief of joy." People perceived as happy, who are enjoying their lives, usually say they have more good in their lives than bad.

There are times when things are so bad, a person may feel as if they don't deserve to enjoy life. A negative act can place enough blame or shame on an individual that their mind tells them they are a bad person who doesn't deserve pleasure. What a lie!

Past Hurts: In my communication sessions, I have coached many people who have been abused and hurt. They sometimes think that people see them as they see themselves: mediocre, passive, uninteresting, insignificant, gross, weak, dumb, unattractive, or ineffective, and their lists are endless. These are their words, not mine. Unfortunately, it comes out in their communication. What's on the inside eventually oozes out. Like toothpaste in a tube, when enough pressure is applied to it, the mixture comes out. Let's look at some examples.

Curtis is a person who sees things his way and only his way. He has a root of anger that his family feels. Every chance he gets, he blows up in a rage. Rarely does he have a considerate and sincere attitude toward those close to him. At his job, he presents well, and his audience may even tell him he did a great job. Even though they compliment him, he doesn't allow himself to enjoy the process nor the compliments.

If a person is trapped in a negative emotion, such as anger, it drives the individual away from enjoyment. It's hard for a person with a root of anger to genuinely enjoy their own successes in life because their vision is obscured. Mostly, all they see is blame or shortcomings in other people. It is up to them to make a decision to work on themselves, take the lock and key off their real emotions, rid themselves of fear, and ask God to help them.

Jessica feels inadequate because she didn't learn proper grammar in school. She has avoided any and all functions in which she might have to write something or even give any type of presentation. She completely avoids communicating to groups of people because she feels they will judge her.

There are plenty of self-help books available in libraries and classes online and in colleges that could help Jessica improve her grammar. Bad grammar is a fixable problem. Once improved, a person can enjoy the process of interacting with others. We all have something to work on. No one is perfect.

Jacob went on an all-inclusive vacation. Hawaii was beautiful to everyone except Jacob. He painted another picture, which was totally the opposite and unrecognizable to the others. His negative tone of voice and his reaction to the environment stunned them. In Jacob's lifetime, he had been confronted with a great deal of disappointment and depression that he, like Curtis, could only see negativity.

In Jacob's case, he should allow himself to view life as it is-the black, white, and gray. This is not easy to say to the individual who has mostly experienced the dark side of life. Yes, there is ugliness in our world, but there is also beauty. We have the power to speak light into dark places. In this case, I am talking about Jacob's mind. My advice for Jacob is to change the channel of his thinking from negativity to positive expectations and confess: "I see life as God sees life." He should confess this at least twenty times a day and deliberately look for beauty in his world, like natural wonders, flowers, the love of friends, and his own existence.

The inner battle is one worth conquering. We all have obstacles and negative situations to deal with, and the key is to not let them deter or destroy us. It is God's desire for us to enjoy life, and this includes the enjoyment of communicating.

> **It is God's desire for us to enjoy life, and this includes the enjoyment of communicating.**

Challenge

What prohibits you from enjoying communicating? What can you do to inject a more contagious atmosphere of enjoyment into your audience and/or those you communicate with?

Declaration

I create an atmosphere of joy and present great knowledge to my audiences and to people on a personal and professional basis when communicating.

- Strategy 10 -

LET YOUR BODY SPEAK

> Now thanks be unto God, which always causeth us to triumph in Christ, and maketh manifest the savior of his knowledge by us in every place.
>
> 2 Corinthians 2:14, King James Version

God's desire is for us all to win in life. In 3 John 1:2 (King James Version) we read, "Beloved, I wish above all things that thou mayest prosper and be in health, even as thy soul prospereth." Along with that, God tells us in Psalm 115:14, "The Lord shall increase you more and more, you and your children." We were born to be winners.

How the Body Speaks

As I purposefully mentioned throughout this book, we communicate in three ways: through our words, nonverbal communication, and spirit. Body language, the nonverbal communication we use, is not only physical gestures, though that is part of it, but a reflection of our spirit—our spirit speaks through our body; it takes over to express what we are communicating. You can easily tell what a person is really saying by reading their body language.

Align Your Languages

When your body speaks, it is vital that your words, tone, and body language match because this unspoken language can enhance or destroy communication. Actions speak louder than words. While someone may question the validity of our words, our body language (posture, locked hand positions, etc.) answers their doubt. When our words match our body language, our audience feels we are believable. When our body language contradicts our words, our credibility may be on the line.

When your body speaks, it is vital that your words, tone, and body language match because this unspoken language can enhance or destroy communication.

Example: Rosa really hurt Michael's feelings. She stood with her hands on her hips and told him that the tuxedo he was wearing was too tight. This was Michael's big day, and he was about to walk into the church and marry the woman of his dreams. Michael, who is overweight, was crushed. Rosa saw the look on his face and apologized saying, she didn't mean to hurt his feelings. Prior to Michael's engagement, he dated Rosa. Michael ended the relationship.

What was Rosa's purpose? When she apologized, do you think she was sincere? Rosa's words and the nonverbal cues contradict each other, causing her credibility and sincerity to be unbelievable.

So, why does the spirit matter? Your spirit communicates to your brain and has purpose. Police say many victims of rape who come in contact with their attackers felt they should have avoided the person. The victims say there was something about the person that didn't feel right. That feeling in your spirit could be God warning you. Some call it intuition, or their "gut," while others refer to this feeling as discernment, a divine warning or word from the Holy Spirit. Whatever terminology you choose to use, we all have a built-in alert system that suggests whether or not we should accept or reject an individual, group, or situation. By listening to your inner communication—your spirit—when someone is speaking, you can quickly decide if you want to be around them, if you can trust them, or if you should run from them. But it takes practice. You must listen and heed those warnings.

Example: When Julie met Donna, right away she felt a strong, positive healthy aura from her. When they talked, they felt they had been friends forever. They really formed a bond and have remained friends as well as business partners. On the other hand, Mark was introduced to a potential client named Paul. Mark was troubled and felt very uncomfortable around Paul. He tried to fight the feelings but could not ignore them. He eventually took Paul on as a client against his better judgment and later learned that Paul had been involved in an illegal activity. His unethical past involvements almost destroyed Mark's reputation and business. Mark learned the hard way to listen to the warnings and guidance of his spirit.

Use Your Eyes

Eye contact is an essential aspect of body language because the eyes reflect emotions such as fear, happiness, and even sadness. They play a critical role in nonverbal communication. For example, when they waiver, they usually indicate guilt, or when they dance and sparkle, they create humor, playfulness, or great joy. William Shakespeare wrote about how the eyes are the windows to the soul. They tell us what we need to know and sometimes what we don't want to know about an individual. Along with our eyes, our eyebrows also communicate messages. When positioned up, they convey a message of deep thought, surprise, or disbelief. When they are pulled down and squinted, the message may be confusion or anger.

Avoiding eye contact is one of the biggest sins in communication, and shyness is no excuse for this behavior. (You will read more about shyness later on in Communication Clinic.) There are many proven ways to overcome shyness, but the easiest is to shift your focus from a person's eyes. Earlier, I shared how looking at the bridge of one's nose makes it seem as if you are looking at the person directly in their eyes but doesn't feel uncomfortable. Remember, a direct and sincere look indicates confidence and will communicate positively to your audience.

Calm Those Nerves

Most people desire to be thought of as confident and effective when they speak, but for many, their body sends a different message because they are nervous. Most likely, these people have been told in school or in family gatherings that they are not good speakers. In many cases, they are simply nervous, and I want to share a solution that will give you amazing results.

The Balancer

Over the years, I have found that people shy away from any form of communicating, especially public speaking, because they believe they look and sound awkward. We know that nonverbal communication speaks louder than verbal communication, and if the verbal and the nonverbal don't match, the nonverbal wins. After watching many speakers and coaching many more, I have developed a proven technique to calm the nervous public speaker, and I call it *The Balancer*.

This diagram explains what happens to people who possess awkward gestures when they speak. People are born three different ways:

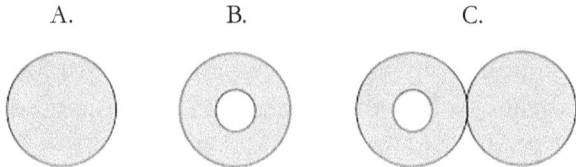

In Diagram A, this shaded circle represents a person who has gestures in check. Diagram B shows there is a circle with an additional inner circle. This person has what I call a hole in their body language. The two adjoining circles in Diagram C show that another person has body language tendencies that connect the individual to circles A and B.

In an actual scenario, person A would speak in front of an audience with ease and flows into the moment with appropriate gestures. The only areas needed for attention here are to make eye contact and know the material being presented and to make sure the person smiles to establish a connection with the audience. Person B, on the other hand, is not grounded. This person's body language can be the center of attention during the presentation. This individual may go into a locked position with their hands being clasped in front or behind or stuck to their sides. This person will also jingle change in their pockets, hold on tight to the podium, use a pointer as a weapon, dance around while delivering their presentation, flap their arms, or produce many other unexpected movements.

I, along with millions of other people, happen to fall into this category. We have this hole in our body language that does not allow us to physically function like person A. I have found the solution to this problem, and it is the reason I created *The Balancer*.

The Balancer satisfies the nerve endings in our body to make us more like person A. I have studied and diagnosed hundreds of clients and found this to be an effective tool. People once scolded as a child and told not to gesture are now set free and communicating with ease. For the first time, they are enjoying life and being heard as a productive member of society.

To determine if a person is a candidate for *The Balancer*, I conduct tests so that I can obtain an actual picture of their body language. My clients are videotaped to show them exactly what many have never seen before. I would like to tell you that more people fall into category A, but this is not true. The majority of people fall into categories B and C.

The C folks are tricky because at different times, they can react as A or B. The goal is to have persons A, B, and C function in a natural state versus an unnatural one.

How does this happen? It's simple. To satisfy the nerves in the body, I simply place *The Balancer*, a pen-like tool, in a person's hand and tell them to hold it as if they are writing. The grip with the second finger acts as a calming agent to the body and replaces the hole in the body language. I am not talking about a click pen. Body type B would click all day long with this. It is important that *The Balancer* be held as prescribed otherwise person B may take the object and beat it on a nearby desk or table. One example of a person who did this is David Letterman. During his Late Night show, you would see him holding a pen in a nonwriting position and from time to time tapping his desk. Remember, *The Balancer* is held as if you were going to write.

With *The Balancer* in place, it is not seen as a distraction while presenting. It is an acceptable tool because it is not uncommon for presenters to jot down notes when interacting with people. Also, as the individual engages the audience, the focus between you and the participants become more heightened.

The Balancer provided life for Ginger. The body language, which was once closed and awkward, was corrected. Ginger was able to gesture freely and openly express herself, and it helped her find her way to confidence in her ability to speak.

I've tested the effectiveness of *The Balancer* by comparing results before and after its use. It unlocks frustration and fills in the hole in the body language that prevents one from functioning freely. It's the one simple tool that gives nervous communicators the confidence they need to succeed in communicating. Go to bonniewinfrey.com for more information on *The Balancer* and how to use it properly.

Control Your Tongue Power

We have tremendous power over life's roadblocks just by using our secret weapon—our tongue. Proverbs 18:21 KJV says, "Death and life are in the power of the tongue." We can speak positive things into existence as well as negative things. Words can encourage, hurt, motivate, compliment, build, heal, love, inspire, offer hope, provide positive self-esteem, promote happiness, educate, entertain, or rob us of self-esteem and destroy the image God originally designed us for, making us feel sad, vulnerable, or unattractive.

We also have the power to speak to roadblocks and mountains in our lives. Jesus said in Matthew 17:20 NKJV, "If you had faith even as small as a mustard seed, you could say to this mountain, 'Move from here to there,' and it would move. Nothing would be impossible." Jesus reiterates this point later by saying in Mark 11:23, "For assuredly, I say to you, whoever says to this mountain, 'Be removed and be cast into the sea,' and does not doubt in his heart, but believes that those things he says will be done, he will have whatever he says." The key here is faith—to believe as little as a mustard seed (one of the smallest seeds, which is only about one or two millimeters in diameter).

When the Enemy Tries to Steal Your Power

As I mentioned above, there is power in the tongue (Proverbs 18:21). I recently spoke to a group of our leaders of the next generation. This annual engagement is one I've enjoyed for about ten years. I love talking to the youth about communication etiquette issues because in my line of work, adults are primarily my clients. So, if I can get to young people and correct some of the bad habits they've learned before they reach adulthood, it will improve the quality of their professional and personal lives.

At one particular event, I wasn't sure I was going to make it because I came down with a really bad upper respiratory infection. I went to my doctor, and he prescribed antibiotics and a decongestant. My body was extremely weak. I had never before experienced this type of sickness at this particular degree. I was determined to speak to this group of youth. On the day of the leadership forum, I felt better so I went.

I was one of four speakers on a panel addressing communication issues. I was the last speaker, and everyone had covered a lot of what I wanted to say. My mouth was very dry prior to the presentation. I thought this was because I hadn't really eaten for a week. My diet consisted of soup, an occasional piece of fruit, and some cranberry juice. I had lost six pounds in that week.

At the conference, I began to drink water that was set out for the speakers. The water was ice cold, not room temperature which is what I recommend for speakers to drink prior to delivering a presentation. I got up after I was introduced, and my mouth completely locked up. My tongue was literally fighting to burst between my lips. They were glued to each other. When I finally got them free, I had to deal with what sounded like smacking. My mouth was traveling faster than my words, similar to a video clip that was not in sync (where the words and the lips don't match). I have never before experienced this type of disaster. As I continued through my presentation, I felt I had two choices. I could have stopped and told the audience what I was experiencing, or I could continue on and try to deliver the information I wanted them to learn. I chose the latter. Here's why. When you tell an audience you are sick or about something physically challenging going on with you, your audience may shift from a learning mode or a participant mode to feeling sorry for you. I wanted this group to be better communicators. If I shifted and went into me, the messages would not have gone forward. It wasn't about me; it was about them.

What was great was that during the Q & A, a question was raised as to how you know when your audience is paying attention to you. At this time, I was able to explain what had happened to me when I was speaking. The great thing about this whole situation was the audience stayed connected to me when I was presenting. They probably thought my lip action was hilarious, but I am sure they received pertinent information to help them become better communicators.

Why did this happen to me? I'm not quite sure. It could have been the medication I was on in combination with the cold water I was drinking.

Let's deal with the reaction from the ego perspective. It's disappointing to know and accept that you didn't nail a presentation, speech, or communication function. We are human beings. We can be competitive, and we want to look and present well. The alternative to beating yourself up is: (1) forgive yourself; (2) let yourself off the hook for having a bad experience; and (3) glean something positive from the situation. This may be difficult because all you see and feel is negative. In my case, I chose to attend and speak at the forum and not use my sickness as an excuse. The students learned valuable information to help improve their communication and were given an open invitation to talk to me should they ever need advice. The enemy wants to tell you that you are ineffective. Don't buy into the lie. Look forward to your next opportunity and expect it to be your best presentation ever. However, if you find yourself feeling ill, then do not attend and contaminate others.

Jayme's husband often tells her that her communication doesn't make sense. She says he complains that she uses the wrong words to express what she is feeling or talking about. Fifty-four-year-old Jayme disagrees, but admits she doesn't have mental clarity at times when she speaks, and she loses interest in her own conversations because she is sometimes unable to concentrate and think clearly.

What can Jayme do to improve her communication? My advice would be to first make sure she understands the meaning of the words she's using. It is advisable to refresh her understanding of words and definitions when there is a doubt about the meanings. I would further advise that she build her vocabulary by investing in a program through a bookstore or the Internet. Another simple way is to read books or to study the dictionary and try to learn at least ten new words a day. Also, Jayme's concentration issues could be related to menopause. She should make an appointment with her physician to rule this out and any other physical or mental issues. My fourth piece of advice for Jayme would be to role-play. She could benefit from putting herself in hypothetical situations that she feels uncomfortable in and create a plan to get through the conversations. For instance, before her husband starts to talk to her, she can develop a plan to keep and/or gain her confidence. When she wants to use a big word, she should learn how the word is used and practice using it alone before presenting it to others.

Have you ever talked to someone and every other word out of their mouth is profanity or slang? It can be very annoying. The reason may be that the person has a lack of vocabulary. Challenge the next person who speaks with a limited vocabulary. The advice I give is to compliment them by saying something like this, "You are intelligent. I know you can talk to me without cursing. Do you curse because you don't know how to express yourself with other words?" The person may become angry but that's okay. I have witnessed profanity and slang diminish to nearly none at all in people I work with.

We have a running joke in my family. On one side of my family, we have mumblers. I actually feel the people are talking very low. My husband always alerts me and asks, "What is he saying?" There is very little tongue action in the speaking process. What is amazing is that the group of people mumbling all understand each other.

There is a difference between talking in a low, quiet tone and mumbling! What's bothersome is that when I speak in a low tone, he is quick to say, "You are mumbling like your family," and that is not true.

If you are a mumbler, make a decision to avoid talking in a low, inarticulate voice. Being a mumbler is always a choice. One can stay in this mode or come out of it. It is just that simple. Once the decision is made to speak clearly, the tongue returns to active status, and the voice level of the person becomes amplified.

If you are a person who stutters, do not give into the lie that you are a bad communicator. You have something worthwhile to say, but unfortunately your words become locked, and they don't come out smoothly. You can overcome this challenge. Let the world hear you! Be free! At least ten times a day you need to stand in front of a mirror and repeat the following affirmation, "I am a great communicator! People love me, and they love to hear me speak." Say these words as powerfully as you can and increase the intensity each time. Then, when you speak, constantly gesture outwardly and watch the words come out of your mouth more freely, and the negative voices inside your head telling you otherwise will eventually go away.

Spend time with yourself and practice, practice, practice speaking. Pull the words out of your head by using your gestures. Don't try to force this to happen. Your hands will automatically help your words flow. You will watch a transformation of how much easier it will be to speak. Another tool you can use in addition to gestures is *The Balancer*.

It is important for all of us to improve ourselves. We are not perfect beings, but one thing we can change and improve is our communication. We should communicate with purpose and determine ahead of time if that purpose is positive or negative. If it is negative, we need to stop our tongue and create a positive way of expression. Once we are sure of the outcome, we should make sure our words and tone match our body language. If they do not, confusion and sometimes irreparable damage results.

Words to Help You Cope

As we journey through life, we encounter roadblocks. They hinder us from reaching our destinations. According to the Cambridge Dictionary, a roadblock is "a temporary structure put across a road to stop traffic." The key word is temporary. Roadblocks in life are given names, such as sickness and disease, death, failures, fear, disasters, ineffective teachers, haters, agitators, financial issues, abuse, rape, prison, divorce, crime, injuries, or any unexpected event or situation that takes you off your perceived course in life.

We can expect the roadblocks and maneuver around them, or we can let them control and defeat us. We have a choice. We can't always control the roadblocks, but we can control our reaction to them. Rage, anger, pain, frustration, or a sense of hopelessness is one option that may temporarily set in. On the other hand, contentment with a plan to detour around them is a far-better alternative course of action.

We can expect the roadblocks and maneuver around them, or we can let them control and defeat us.

I often say that God brings people into our life to help us cross the finish line, and my prayer partner, Janice, is one of those angels. She has taught me so much when it comes to dealing with the challenges of life. Nothing seems to bother her. When she is confronted with a roadblock, her reply to it is, "It's all good." The stress leaves her and upon speaking those words, she immediately surrenders the circumstances or situations over to God.

I was once given a plaque as a gift, and it read, "Lord, help me to remember that nothing is going to happen to me today that You and I together can't handle," re-phrased from Philippians 4:13 that says, "I can do all things through Christ who strengthens me." That plaque's message is priceless. I would love to thank whoever wrote it, but on the plaque, it says it was an old preacher's greeting to each new day. I refer to it as Psalm 91 in a nutshell.

When the pressures of life seems extremely difficult, you can simply say, "This is a job for God," and it helps tremendously. It is important to totally surrender the problem to God and let Him work it out.

When challenged, be prepared to repeat these statements in order to obtain the peace you desire. For instance, if I am confronted with a challenging situation, I may say, "God and I can handle this," and repeat it three more times until I realize that I am not in the problem by myself. Pressure dissipates, and I go on with the rest of the day. In the end, the situation is better, and most of the time, I am blessed beyond my expectations.

Just Sleep on It

When life gets really heavy, go to sleep. It is no mistake that there are twenty-four hours in a day. Sleep refreshes and restores us for the activities of the next day. Sleep is also a prescription given by physicians to simply heal the body of mental and physical stress.

Again, your spirit speaks through your body. If your spirit is tired, weak, beat up, fearful, or anxious, your audience will hear its voice way above your spoken words, so in addition to preparing your words, prepare your body.

Challenge

In which area do you feel most confident, with your words, nonverbal communication, or your spirit? Practice using *The Balancer*. How can you include *The Balancer* in your next presentation? Learning from mistakes is often a painful but memorable lesson. What have you learned about overcoming roadblocks and derailments?

Declaration

I am ready to face my giants, and I accept my strengths and weaknesses as I develop my new skills. I am a capable and creative speaker. The stage is mine and I'm going to enjoy it!

Communication Clinic

*Real-Life Scenarios and Prescriptions for Learning
How to Earn the Applause You Deserve!*

Now that we've looked at ten communication strategies to help present our best self as we command our world, let's bring it all together. In this final section, I've provided scenarios I've encountered, and I know you can learn from them to improve your skills. I've also developed several prescriptions that will help you work through both general and specific issues involving communication. Use this chapter as a mirror and take an honest look at your body language, words, and your delivery, asking yourself, "How can I handle each situation?"

Master the Waves:
Real-Life Scenarios to Test Your Skills

Below are scenarios from people I have met and counseled. I include them here to provide you with proven solutions and techniques you can use in every type of communication in which you engage.

The Shy, Hesitant Leader
Meet Joe, an engineer who supervises approximately twenty-five people and has a difficult task ahead of him. He has been instructed to reprimand members of his crew for not doing their job properly. Joe is known for looking down at the floor when he is talking to his group. How can you help Joe overcome this problem?

Joe may either be shy or feels threatened by his group, or Joe just doesn't know how to communicate or reprimand in an effective manner. Some people feel badly when they have to deliver news from higher up and fail to convey the message, or they beat themselves up while they reprimand others, and it comes through in their body language and words. Here is a teaching moment. The best way to help Joe is to follow his eye contact before he gets to the floor, or comes up from floor, and connect with his eyes. While connecting, raise your eyes to an upward position, which should ensure Joe that it is okay to have a face-to-face encounter. This gesture is usually exaggerated. Sometimes the person will attempt to go back to the floor, but continue the process, and you'll eventually help Joe overcome this problem.

This works because you are teaching Joe how to connect and communicate with others. This act is also helping him to gain confidence while speaking. Joe now feels he has someone who wants to listen to him and someone who values what he is talking about. The world is full of Joes.

The Snarky Superior
Nancy, a registered nurse, is sent out to interview physicians about what they feel the future role for nurses will include. With every question, Nancy is cut off. One physician played the authoritative role, took over her interview, and redirects questions to Nancy, asking her what she feels her role should be. The physician went on to imply that the role will be the same as it presently is: to carry out the physician orders as specified. Nancy was rattled during this interview process and didn't ask any further questions. It's obvious that she didn't handle this situation properly. What could she have done?

Nancy's first problem was she didn't anticipate the good, the bad, or the ugly of what could happen in an interview. She wasn't prepared to be shut down. There are a few things Nancy could have done to turn this process around in her favor:

> 1. **Be prepared.** Know your subject matter and the climate in which you are speaking, and be prepared for negatives as well as positives in your interview. Do your homework ahead of time. We talked about this in *Strategy 4, Understand Your Environment.*

2. **Greet the interviewees with a smile and a firm handshake.** This shows you are in control.

3. **Put aside your shyness.** No one has to know you have a weakness when it comes to speaking. Overcome your shyness by moving out of your comfort zone and addressing individuals with direct eye contact and a stable voice.

4. **Adjust your rate of speaking, volume, and vocal tone.** The one mistake that communicators make when speaking to someone who intimidates them is to slow down their speech, soften their voices, and change their tone of talking from friendly and conversationally to a more passive one. This is not the time to pause and let the dominant person run over you. Remain in control by talking conversationally with a volume that is not too soft or too loud, and speak at a rate that is easily understood—not too fast and not too slow.

5. **Watch your posture.** Whatever you do, if you are seated, don't change your posture from leaning forward to leaning back in a chair to taking your arm and placing it toward the back of the chair. This is a cue to the interviewee that they are in control, and they gain ground over you. This is a good way to set yourself up as mincemeat. If you are standing, avoid taking a step back or leaning backward if the other party is dominating the conversation. It has the same effect.

Could Nancy have recovered and regained control of her interview? Of course, all she had to do was to lean forward, use direct eye contact, and redirect the question with a somewhat firmer, yet friendly and conversational tone. She could have responded to the physician's comments with, "Okay, that's not exactly the response I was looking for." The tone of the conversation would have instantly changed, and the offending physician would have recognized that Nancy was back in control.

The Cold Reception
John represents a company that is investigating illegal practices of a facility. He must interview the facility's management team and, based

upon his findings, recommend to his superiors whether or not the facility should be closed.

John walks in and greets the interviewees with a smile, handshakes, and a friendly greeting. However, the management staff appear cold and evasive. It is obvious to John that he is not welcome at this facility. How should he respond to this cold reception?

    1. **Don't change.** Stay warm, friendly, and conversational, but be direct with your questions and allow adequate time for the management staff to respond.

    2. **Try to get the interviewees to relax.** This can be done by not compromising who you are. Lay out your purpose for being there on the table. Sometimes this helps to calm anxiety, unless the interviewee is deliberately covering up information. Inform staff that this is an investigation, not an indictment.

    3. **Don't give in to intimidation.** Stay in control of the interview process and don't give in to the negative or defensive atmosphere. It doesn't matter if the people aren't happy about you being in their facility. You have a job to do.

    4. **Stay focused and stick to the issues at hand.** It's common to feel rejected when launching an investigation of this type. Although this is common, it is not wise. Don't take it personally; just do your job.

Prescription to Get Rid of Low Self-Esteem

Now, if you are a person with low self-esteem, don't own negative, demeaning thoughts, which I call daggers, that are being thrown at you every day to destroy you. Recreate who you are. Know that you were created by God for greatness and that you can do anything.
On a daily basis say, "I am loved by God, and I can do all things through Christ who strengthens me." You've got to believe in yourself! Remember the song I mentioned earlier from the soundtrack, The Wiz entitled, "Believe in Yourself"? The lyrics from one of the verses goes like this:

> You've got to believe in yourself right from the start.
> You've got to believe in the magic right there in your heart.
> Believe all these things, not because I told you to. Go ahead, believe in yourself! Believe in yourself!
> Believe in yourself as I believe in you.

God wants us to believe in ourselves as He believes in us. We need to know who we are in Christ. When we know who we are, our self-esteem increases, and the negative messages and lies that play in our minds tend to diminish.

When we know who we are, our self-esteem increases, and the negative messages and lies that play in our minds tend to diminish.

To rid low self-esteem, here is a prescription that will solve the problem:

1. **Stand in front of a mirror and speak these affirmations:** "God loves me. I am beautiful/handsome. I love to talk to people, and they love to be around me and communicate with me." Repeat these affirmations at least ten times a day. Also, remember what the Bible says, "I can do all things through Christ who strengthens me" (Philippians 4:13).

2. **Commit to doing something nice for someone every single day.** Volunteer to give a senior citizen some help. Go to an organization that seeks volunteers and offer your assistance. Help a family member who can't help themselves. By focusing on someone else and complimenting others, this will help you feel good about yourself.

3. **Develop a sense of style that presents a new you.** This doesn't mean you have to spend a lot of money on clothing. Rearrange what you have in your closet. Care about your clothes and how

you wear them. Make sure they are clean and pressed. If you are dressing as though you are in the nineteenth century, you should buy some twenty-first century pieces. If you lack in the area of grooming, clean your body, shave, comb, and cut (if needed) and style your hair. The point is, when one grooms and dresses, you feel better about yourself, and that impression is felt among those who surround you.

4. **Change your posture.** Pull yourself from the top of your head, as if there is a giant string elongating you. A true sign of low self-esteem (unless there is a medical problem or cultural issue) is a person who looks down and has slumped shoulders. Look people directly in the eye or eye area. Walk with a new attitude. Put some pep in your step. Energy helps to produce self-confidence.

5. **Motivate yourself. Get a theme song.** If you don't have one, borrow mine or you can google one of your own or purchase one on iTunes. Another way is to listen to great motivational speakers. Their messages should prompt you to act. You can also be your own motivator; simply put words and music together and create your own theme song about yourself. List your positive attributes or everything you desire to be and add some upbeat music to it. Sing it daily and love yourself. If this song doesn't make you smile, go back to the drawing board and recreate until the words and tune produce a smile.

6. **Look for opportunities to shake someone's hand.** When you connect, this should be a firm handshake. A sure sign of defining a person with low self-esteem is to shake their hand and feel their weak, limp handshake. This is a clue that a person may have something to hide, or they are timid. Stay firm even if the other person's handshake is weak.

7. **Exercise is a sure way to build self-esteem.** Many times, insecurity is brought on because a person is overweight, underweight,

or ashamed of their personal appearance. When one exercises, you are doing something for yourself to improve your health and overall physical appearance. Exercise also creates energy and makes you feel good. This motivation may help you accomplish goals. Success breeds success.

8. **Use Scripture.** When fear arises, repeat verses like this, "God has not given me a spirit of fear and timidity, but of power, love, and self-discipline" (2 Timothy 1:7). "I will fear no evil: for thou art with me; thy rod and thy staff they comfort me" (Psalms 23:3 KJV). "No weapon that is formed against thee shall prosper" (Isaiah 54:17). Be bold as a lion and remember lions don't have to roar. They know who they are.

9. **Improve your quality of voice.** Do you speak too softly? If so, use your deep tones. If you speak very boisterous, tame your tone. If you speak too fast, you must slow down. If you communicate too slowly, use inflections and add energy into the conversation. (See Strategy 4 for more details on voice quality.)

10. **Look for opportunities to fight fear**. When asked to present to an audience, take the challenge. In a crowded room, don't sit in the back; move and sit closer to the front. When the inner voice says that you are ineffective as a communicator (and it will), confront and dismantle that lie by setting a goal to communicate successfully. Counter by saying, "I am a fantastic speaker!"

Prescription for Overcoming Shyness

There is a force that restricts us and prevents us from taking advantage of opportunities. It keeps one from approaching others. It definitely hates the spotlight, and it's called shyness. Shyness can grow up in an individual and rob a person of venturing out and experiencing life to the fullest.

When I was young, there was a youth director at my church that no one really messed with. She specialized in the ability to single out quiet, shy children and scare the wits out of them. I was one of those victims, and I do mean victim. I was quiet, shy, and kept to myself.

Ms. Ida would pull me to her and say, "I have a speech for you." My heart sank every time she approached me. It was always a mistake to tell her "no" because she never took it for an answer. Year after year throughout my childhood she would make me get in front of our church and deliver speeches. I literally hated it. But what did I really hate? Was it that I was made to do something I didn't want to do? Was it because I was really terrified? Was it that I didn't like being around other people other than the ones I selected? Or was it that I was being pushed to exit my comfort zone? The answer to all these questions is "yes"!

She saw greatness in me that I couldn't see or feel. God used her to prepare me for my purpose and destiny in life. The speeches got easier. Did I like them? No. The speeches turned into talks and announcements, and it didn't take long before I began to feel more comfortable delivering them. At the same time, I caught a glimpse of my future. At our church, the members have always been supportive, so when people came up to me with a compliment, I felt it was routine and something they told everyone. But when people outside of my church family heard me speak and their remarks were the same, I began to embrace and accept the compliments.

I was one of many children Ms. Ida helped to nurture and step into their purpose. I often compare this revelation learned to one of my 5K races. At the beginning of one particular race, I wasn't feeling well and didn't know why. Still, I was determined to run. It had stormed all day, and the race was threatened by lightning and scattered thunderstorms. Finally, an hour before the race, organizers announced the race would proceed. I psyched myself up and took off with the rest of the runners. Toward the end, I started feeling lethargic. Fellow runners ran up near me to tell me that I was dehydrated and to drink some water. The atmosphere and the run were both challenging me. It was interesting when one of my sons ran to me from the finish line side and yelled, "Mom, you can do this; speed it up!" For him, I did. He ran alongside of me up to the finish line.

As I approached the finish line, supporters and fellow runners who had already crossed were cheering and yelling. I, too, was yelling. I noticed my son off to the side. He had moved away so that I could cross the finish line alone.

All of sudden, it dawned on me that God sends people in our lives to help us cross the finish line in life. That is what my son demonstrated to me. The purpose of this book is to help communicators around the globe know they can be effective. That is also who the late Ms. Ida was in my life. She taught me that shyness was not an excuse to avoid becoming the woman God called me to be.

Prescription to Challenge Obstacles with Confidence

Take the brakes off your limitations. Sometimes we set ourselves up for failure, like Anna who recently went to court. She received a traffic violation she felt she didn't deserve. She didn't want to pay the fine because she didn't have the money to pay what she thought was an outrageous amount. When she arrived, intimidation met her there. Police officers walked around the room with serious facial expressions, and one officer was even holding his hand near his holster. She was frightened, and the people around her appeared to be similarly intimidated. Court was the last thing Anna wanted to experience; she felt doomed and knew she would lose her case. Questions rushed through her mind. Why did I come? Why didn't I just borrow the money to pay the ticket? She wanted to escape the courtroom.

Finally, her name was called. The judge, dressed in black, called her to his bench with a bang of his gavel. He then proceeded to ask her if she was guilty of the charges. In a meek voice and with slumped posture she replied, "No, your Honor." He went on to tell her what was reported as the traffic offense and asked her if she could explain to him what happened. Anna was consumed with terror. In a slight whisper, she told the judge that she didn't run the red light in question. The judge said, "Well, our video says differently." He then asked her if she wanted to see the video. Anna declined. The judge then ordered her to pay the fine plus court costs.

The irony behind this situation is Anna was actually not guilty. If she had looked at the video, she would have noticed that she started her turn into the intersection when the light was yellow and only after she passed through most of the intersection did the light turn red. Anna could have used the video in her defense, and her argument should have been that she was wrongly trapped by the cameras as a person who ran a red light. She and the judge only focused on her vehicle. He asked her if she owned the vehicle in question with said license plates and she did.

What went wrong here? First of all, Anna convicted herself before she arrived in court. Even though she said she wanted the case dismissed in her favor, her negative body language and lack of appropriate communication sent the opposite message.

What could have been the outcome if Anna's mental expectation hadn't been that of defeat? Take Joni for instance; when she walked up to the judge as her name was called, everyone present could see and feel her confidence. In a cheerful voice, she said, "Good morning, Judge Harper." He proceeded to read off her charges and then asked for her plea. She immediately said, "Not guilty, Your Honor." Once again, he directed her to the video, which was at the same intersection as Anna's clocked vehicle.

Judge Harper told Joni that the tape indicated she ran the red light. Joni then said, "Judge Harper, I hate to differ with you, but I am not guilty." The judge replied as he did with Anna, stating that the video supported the charge. Joni advised the judge that she was concerned when she heard the news that she had been charged with this offense. She went back to the intersection to see how this could have happened. She told the judge she watched many cars nabbed by the automated cameras. "I actually took my own video to show how your system has a malfunction. Each of these vehicles that I am going to show you were all in the right as I was. They all proceeded into the intersection with the light displaying yellow, and after the vehicles made their turns, the light went to red. Now, Judge Harper, how did this happen?" Joni continued to look him in the eye and stated, "I am not guilty, Your Honor."

The judge chuckled and said, "That's a fine piece of PI work; case dismissed."

What was the difference in the two cases? The different body language, for sure; one lacked confidence and the other one screamed it. Anna felt contained within the box (system), whereas Joni decided to challenge the system. The two outcomes were different; one was of defeat, and the other was to win. Winning begins in our minds.

Winning begins in our minds.

Prescription for Handling Adversarial Situations

Even though God wants us to prosper, there is someone who doesn't. Mankind's enemy, satan, works very hard to keep us from communicating effectively and would love for all of us to fail in life. The key to defeating him is to understand his modus operandi or mode of operation (MO). His major purpose is to kill, steal, and destroy us (see John 10:10). Expect adversarial situations before you encounter a victory. The enemy comes to knock you off your game and to try to get you to doubt and refocus your attention.

In Strategy 3, we looked at a variety of personality types that I labeled, "enemy," but I want to reiterate here that our only real enemy on earth is not human—he is the devil, and he works through human beings. In Ephesians 6:12, we are given God's armor to protect us from this enemy, and we're reminded, "For we do not wrestle against flesh and blood, but against principalities, against powers, against the rulers of the darkness of this age, against spiritual hosts of wickedness in heavenly places." There is a very real and active war between good and evil. It takes determination to not only pay attention to enemy fire, but to overcome it. Let's look at one common scenario and see if it is handled correctly.

Jason was chosen by his company to give a presentation to stockholders. He decided he would take the day off before his speech to polish his presentation. His wife was at work, and the house was a mess. He cleaned the entire house. He went out in the evening and came back and saw that the counter in the kitchen was dirty. He asked his wife, "Who did this?" She snapped and said, "Just because you cleaned up, you think it is a big deal!" This saddened Jason because he spent three hours cleaning the whole house. Later that night, he walked into another room (one he had cleaned as well) and noticed that his wife was lying on the couch with an empty glass of what appeared to have been wine. She was asleep with nuts all over her, the sofa, and the floor. He woke her up and advised her to go to bed and she did, but the mess was still in place. Jason was fuming with anger and feeling very hurt.

He then thought, This is a trick of the enemy to move me away from keeping a healthy mindset and drag me down into disappointment and rage. With that thought, Jason decided to leave the mess for his wife to clean and instead diverted his attention to achieving his goal at his upcoming presentation.

When Jason decided to switch the direction of his thinking, the rage was replaced with new feelings, his focus changed, and he began to concentrate more on his prep and the successful day he was going to experience. Jason knew and realized the trick of the enemy. The temptation was to go into the negative, but Jason decided to not let the enemy gain victory over his mind.

When dealing with adversarial situations, refocus from the negative mindset as Jason did, and tap into positive energy. Redirect the verbal to engage in the goal or purpose. For example, in Jason's case, he could have said, "My presentation is going to be the best I've ever given."

Prescription for Handling Your Mistakes

We must win when communicating, even though we make mistakes. Humans are not perfect. Sometimes we have to accept failure on our part, and if things do not turn out as we plan, we have to get over them and go on and try to make better choices. We can grow from our mistakes. This is when character comes into play. When you make a mistake, do you just ignore it or do you confront and deal with it? Sometimes we have to accept failure on our part. The first step is to acknowledge it for what it is. Sometimes guilt can enlarge a situation and blow it out of perspective. A mistake is simply an error, a misunderstanding, or misconception. The outcome of rectifying a situation may not be a positive one, but the winning aspect—acknowledging a situation—frees you of guilt, an all-consuming emotion.

The outcome of rectifying a situation may not be a positive one, but the winning aspect—acknowledging a situation—frees you of guilt, an all-consuming emotion.

Scenario 1

Lisa is a person who tries to keep her word. She made an appointment at her nail salon. Unfortunately, when the two weeks rolled around for her to go, she didn't. She couldn't remember if the appointment was for Monday or Tuesday, and she knew she should have called to confirm the day and time, but she chose to ignore the appointment. Every day from that point on, she was consumed with condemnation. You have to know that Lisa values being a person of her word. She loved this establishment and felt she cost two nail technicians money—one for her manicure and the other for a pedicure. Week three rolled, around and she really needed to go in for the service. She was faced with the options of calling and making an appointment with her regular salon or going to another facility. Since she loved the service where she normally went, Lisa chose to call to get in with her normal technicians.

When she arrived, all she could think about was how to make the wrong right. Her first thought was to pay the technicians what she cost them for not showing up. The problem was she didn't have the money to do so. She finally decided not to ignore the missed appointments and be honest and simply apologize. She did. To her surprise, both technicians told her that they didn't know what she was talking about, and that it was all right. Lisa walked out of the establishment with a burden lifted off of her and a realization that if she hadn't opened her mouth, guilt would have taken her over to the point of where it would have contained her and possibly stopped her from eventually returning to that particular business.

Scenario 2

Jordan and his wife, Michelle, were in the process of getting a divorce. Michelle, a really hard worker, had been bringing in most of the money. Jordan worked here and there and enjoyed sitting back on Michelle's income. Michelle preferred Jordan have steady employment, but this had not been his choice. What he did with his free time was break their marriage vows by having a couple of affairs.

When Michelle learned of the infidelities, she wanted out of the marriage. She felt used and betrayed. Jordan had a choice to make: to fight for his family or not. The interesting part was, when peeling away the hurt, they both said they still loved each other. They separated.

Later, the two decided to give their marriage another try. Jordan admitted to Michelle that he was wrong for having the affairs and that he loved her and only her. He also begged for her forgiveness but said he resented her for being the financial strength in the family. He then declared he would go and find a job to support the family. He also decided he wanted to go to counseling to become a better person, husband, and father to their three children.

Scenario 3

Jonathan was fired from his job. Management decided to conduct a random drug test. Jonathan, unfortunately, came up unclean. A decision at a wild party the night before led to a mistake that took away his income for his family. Three years later, Jonathan has not been able to find a job of the same caliber and income level. This one mistake damaged his self-esteem, his marriage, and his career.

Jonathan had a choice to make; to get back in the saddle or just settle. He decided to first seek forgiveness from his family and from himself. Then he decided to find an attorney to help him plead for an expungement of his record. The outcome was successful, and Jonathan now has a better job than the one he had originally.

In all three of these scenarios, three steps occurred:

1. Acknowledgment of the situation
2. Forgiveness or an attempt to try to forgive
3. A plan set in motion to rectify the mistake

Remember to keep your communication clear and concise when acknowledging a mistake. Let's go back and review a practical approach for Scenario 1. "Vivian, I am so sorry that I missed an appointment with you. I try not to miss my appointments. In the future, I will call you if I don't remember the exact date and time of my appointments, so I can cancel or postpone if necessary. Please forgive me." Note: In the first scenario, the technicians let Lisa off the hook when she said she was sorry and also asked her why she was sorry. They told her it was okay, and the situation was rectified.

In Scenario 2, it was crucial for Jordan to realize what he had done to himself and his family. It was not a case that was going to be pushed under the rug. His life, as he knew it, was destroyed. He owned up to what he had done by saying, "Michelle, I am so sorry for hurting you. I don't know what came over me. I need some help. You are the best thing that has ever happened to me. I don't deserve you. I have treated you badly. I may never forgive myself, but will you try to forgive me? I really want our marriage to work and would do anything, including counseling, to help us get back together."

After some time had passed, Michelle agreed to work on the marriage.

Scenario 3 could have ruined Jonathan's career. After he acknowledged what he had done and forgave himself, he was able to make the necessary plans to rectify the problem. He went to an attorney and pleaded his case. "Attorney Milder, I have made a huge mistake and I need your help. I have worked on my job for fifteen years, and I have only missed three days of work and those were when my children were born. I met up with some old college buddies and we were drinking, and I indulged in drugs. I gave drugs up years ago. One night changed my life into a nightmare. I heard you are one of the best attorneys to get advice from in reference to an expungement. Please help me."

The attorney helped and the expungement was granted.

God makes provision for our sins and our mistakes. The enemy's plan is to condemn and contain us. If he can diminish who we are supposed to be, he's happy. God says He gives us life so that we will live it more abundantly.

Prescription for Overcoming Insecurity

Do you remember Barry from *Strategy 2: It's All about Them: Navigating the Pride Trap*? Though it looks as if pride was his main problem (the need to be the center of attention, refusing to apologize, unwilling to accept criticism, etc.), insecurity was what fueled his abrasive behavior.

Barry's past surfaced every time someone confronted him. Just as he worked hard to keep his family secret, he works harder to keep his mask in place. It is his protection. That is why, when someone confronts him and uses the word you, he immediately starts blaming. Barry is very insecure, and his behavior cannot be trusted. Are you Barry? If the word *you* hurts, follow these steps—you can be helped!

1. Admit this word is offensive.

2. Allow and give yourself permission to be loved and accepted.

3. Forgive whoever hurt you in the past. Don't allow your mind to replay the negative experience. The word *you* acts as a trigger to send you back to the pain even though you may or may not remember.

4. Know that you have the power and choice to accept or reject what anyone says to you.

5. Decide to judge yourself honestly and forgive yourself.

6. Find someone you trust to be accountable to. It must be someone who has your best interest at heart.

7. Accept new people in your life. Don't scare away people because they want to be close or get to know you. Believe it or not, not everyone wants to hurt you.

8. Seek good counseling if you are consumed and can't get past hurts that haunt you.

9. Give yourself permission to live a life free from bondage.

10. Move on!

Prescription for Success

Remember Ginger? We last talked about her in *Strategy 10: Let Your Body Speak*. She made it through her presentation, overcame her fears, wowed her audience, won over the clients, and saved her company millions of dollars, thanks to her plan. She is now called on by her boss to present on many top level projects. She's come a long way from not wanting to be around people. Ginger's no different from any of us; she recognized she had a lack and wanted to improve. Accept this prescription and watch it work for you:

> 1. Repeat affirmations ten times a day because they have a way of getting to the subconscious and overriding negativity. Affirmation statements are about the present. Turn your lack or shortcomings into a positive by creating an "I am" statement. Think big! For instance, you would never say, "I was beautiful/handsome" or "I will be beautiful/handsome," but instead say, "I am beautiful/handsome." The past is over, and the future hasn't arrived. Both keep you from entering into the present.

> Increase your intensity and aggressiveness as you continue saying the affirmations. As a result, you will change, and the outcome will be more confidence and a joy for speaking. Your audiences will feed off your positive energy and enjoy your presentations.

> 2. Study the ten strategies presented in this book. Be a successful, effective communicator. Our Creator made us communicators. Own up to the challenge of being confident.

> 3. If you are a candidate for The Balancer mentioned in **Strategy 10**, do not hesitate; use it and witness the remarkable improvement in your communication. If you are a borderline candidate, please use it to guarantee your security. The Balancer will put your body language into a total healing state.

> 4. Last but not least, pray! People who fear communicating (presenting) sometimes feel like murmuring the words spoken in the Wizard of Oz, "Lions, tigers, bears, oh my!" But this simple prayer will help to eradicate fear. Before any presentation or training session I pray these words, and they work:

> *Dear God:*
> *Thank You for this opportunity to speak (or train). Let this be the best presentation (or training session) I have ever done. Speak through me. Ease any anxiety I may be feeling. Open the ears and understanding of all those in attendance. Let us have a great experience together. In Jesus' name, Amen.*

Then, I deal with the butterflies in my stomach by walking around in an unoccupied area. Walking helps relieve the stress. After that, I reaffirm out loud or silently, "This is going to be the best presentation I've ever given." As with each presentation you deliver, expect to get better each time, and you will continually improve and outdo yourself.

Command, Engage, and Win!

When your body speaks, does it tell you anything? Well, if you ask Frances, an older woman who works in a Georgia hospital who has learned the truth, she would certainly say it does. Frances has been known for tracking the actions of those around her. After a person speaks or commits an act out of character, it is not uncommon to hear her use the phrase with her southern accent, "Does that tell you anything?" Frances knows the body speaks volumes and doesn't hesitate to point it out to others.

In this world, we have dominion over this earth. What are you called to do in life? Which mountain will you conquer? Own your mountain and be the master of influence for which you were designed. With this world being our stage, we have been given a great opportunity to set it, own it, and enjoy it. We have the gift of command. The power of your spoken voice changes and inspires lives, champions greatness as well as battles, and transforms programming from negative to positive in one's mind.

Engage your influence and power. Make your environment a better place because you rule and reign. Your words have power and influence. Your words can take you on a journey to experience life or death, poverty or prosperity, or mediocrity or failure. For instance boxer-great, humanitarian, Muhammad Ali, who died at the age of seventy-four was known for calling himself "the greatest." He spoke it into existence. His talent and abilities mimicked his words. When he died on June 3, 2016, as you clicked through the television channels, all you heard was him being referenced as "the greatest."

Here's another example of owning what you say. Milton often spoke and joked about how he needed to die before his insurance switched over to a less-beneficial policy in which he had to pay more. The day before the policy expired, he passed away.

There are no limits to what you can create. Activate change! Activate your dreams! Find your voice and tell your story! Present your best self and earn the applause you deserve. The applause (whether heard or internally recognized) builds confidence and is an outward expression of victory and winning. Command and engage your influential power and win!

We win by using positive words to create our world. We win when we listen to God and learn to discern the spiritual forces around and in us. We win when our communication and our body language agree and speak the same message with no contradictions. In this world where communicating is so crucial, we have the power to encourage others, educate, recreate our world, and even love at the highest levels.

After reading *Command Your World*, it is my dream and desire that everyone will enjoy and appreciate this priceless gift and power called communication. Just as the Ten Commandments in the Bible gives us guidelines about living on earth, the ten strategies in this book are here to help you polish and maximize your skills as well as keep your audiences wanting more.

I'd like to leave you with this visualization. At the end of my personal presentations (depending on the subject matter and audience), I generally throw a plastic hamburger bun to the audience and say, "If you worked at a restaurant and someone ordered a hamburger, is this all you would give them? No, you would pile on the lettuce, a couple slices of tomato, meat, and condiments" (all are thrown out as named to the audience). I end by saying, "Give your audiences, your friends, co-workers, and family everything you have." Every time you speak and listen, give of yourself and enjoy this amazing journey called communication.

Finally, Patti LaBelle, in a concert while singing, "Somewhere over the Rainbow," paused at the end and finished the song with these powerful lyrics:

"If a teeny weeny bird can fly over the rainbow; then why, oh why, can't I?"

That has been the message of *Command Your World*: you can! Now, spread your wings and f-l-y!

COMMUNICATION CLINIC

When God said, "Let there be light," He believed it, saw it, spoke it, and it happened. God has used me to see what others can't see within themselves. Through Him, I assess a person's communication strengths and weaknesses, and through Him, I give them the prescription they need to polish their skills and be successful.

I am thankful for the opportunity to train in the area of communications. Below, I have shared a few comments regarding previous communication training sessions.

Overcomers Speak Out

Bonnie, you received the highest scores of any consultant we have hired to teach our surveyors. You received universal praise by the students for your knowledge of the subject matter, your ability to communicate in a manner that was understood, your ability to relate the material to specific jobs so that it became meaningful, your willingness to spend additional time with people who needed or requested it, and your deft facilitation. You were commended for these same things by those who observed your teaching. When you began at the Joint Commission, it was teaching in the hospital program—I think as a pilot test. But by word of mouth, your reputation grew so that people began requesting you, and you were teaching in all the accreditation programs.

N. Deal Chandler
Former Vice President of the Joint Commission

Bonnie Winfrey invariably demonstrates the amazing life-changing impact she has on the participants of the Distinguished Young Women of Illinois Scholarship Program. By teaching them to defy complacency, to face their fears and take calculated risks, to use obstacles that come in their path as stepping stones, and to use their innate mental and emotional strength to choose their own path, she guides them to be a force for good and live a life of purpose. She has been invaluable to the success of this leadership program.

Mohra Gavankar
Distinguished Young Women of D.C. Chair

A large group of medical professionals (e.g., physicians, nurses, administrators, and pharmacists) were gathered for their new position orientation and training course. Even though these individuals came from diverse educational and professional backgrounds, they were hired to perform the same job duties. A significant aspect of their new job involved interviewing and communicating with healthcare workers, working in all job classifications within healthcare institutions. Even though these individuals considered themselves strong communicators prior to the exercise, they found Bonnie's tips extremely valuable.

Catherine Norins
Former Joint Commission Supervisor

Bonnie, it is with pleasure that I write this; however, it does not come close to expressing how special you are and how great you are at what you do. Being a part of the Communications Clinic with Bonnie provided me with clear, objective feedback on how to more effectively communicate with others. Bonnie is very observant and has a natural talent for analyzing her subject. She understands that a dynamic presentation that captivates an audience takes work from the inside out. Bonnie displays a genuine interest in you as an individual and optimizes your strengths while giving you a personal mantra, when necessary, to build confidence in the areas that need improvement. She even follows up with your progress. Bonnie has equipped me with tools that I use in every encounter of my day. It was really a joy working with Bonnie, and I highly recommend her communications training.

Denene Harper
American Hospital Association

What I liked about the interview clinic was the instructor and her approach to the session—very knowledgeable and supportive. Tops! Best program of this sort I've even seen.

Tate Treat
Joint Commission Surveyor

Bonnie's communications training has definitely impacted my life. I am a better communicator because of her training. I have compiled a list, which I refer to as "Bonnie's Words of Wisdom." Before speaking, I review the list. This is my pep talk that gets me ready and hyped for the challenge of presenting technical information. This list also contains practical solutions for dealing with speaker anxiety as well as the mental and physical preparation needed for being a great speaker. I will be forever grateful to Bonnie for intuitively knowing what I needed and challenging me to always give my best.

Anita Rapier
American Hospital Association

I completed Bonnie's communication training seminar, and I must say that it has had a huge impact on the way I now conduct my presentations. Before, my presentations were just lackluster and, well, boring. After implementing some of the tips and ideas that Bonnie suggested, I have improved 100%. I feel more comfortable, I'm more prepared, and I actually feel excited about presenting the material. The information that Bonnie gives is very personalized to the individual. She was able to tell me things about the way I feel when I'm presenting that I knew to be true but had never told her. As a result, she works by giving you information that will help you grow as an individual and not just general information about how to present the information. I enjoyed the training tremendously and truly believe that I would not be the much-improved presenter that I am now without it.

Gretchen Young-Charles
American Hospital Association

Bonnie was one of the first people to see potential in me. I remember her walking up to me telling me that I should compete in pageants. I never thought that I had the ability to do it. Through her trainings, she has instilled confidence and courage in me to pursue my dreams. Outside of pageantry, she pushes me to envision a life greater than myself. There was a moment in my life where I wanted to leave the tech industry but she helped me combine all of my passions in order for me to reach my fullest potential. Her training not only helped me through pageantry and navigating the tech industry, but also in everyday life.

Rita Roloff, Top 15 at Miss WIUSA
Software Developer on Wall Street Creator of: "Bold Steps, Big Difference"

I had the pleasure and opportunity to work closely with Bonnie Winfrey during several provider training seminars. She provided essential provider education and instructional training. Bonnie was very familiar with communication techniques and incorporated our specific evaluation standards and assessment requirements into her training sessions.

The most impressive aspect of Bonnie's trainings was her innate ability to provide critical positive critiques and suggestions on how to successfully manage provider interaction. She is in a league of her own. Bonnie's technique is the model for effective communication. She has a wonderful and easy demeanor. Bonnie is very knowledgeable. She presented information on a variety of topics. She even provided extra instructional support based on individual assessments. Bonnie projects a positive presence and has a remarkable sense of humor.

Bonnie is an excellent contribution to any corporation's training program.

Octavia Browder-Winston
Manager of Operations -Texas Healthcare Alliance

Closing Note from the Author:

It is my desire that from this book, you will experience the same results as the aforementioned attendees of my Communication Clinics. I hope the tools and suggestions mentioned throughout each strategy will increase your knowledge and power, make you a better communicator, help you earn the applause you deserve, and keep your audience wanting more.

You have the power to create and build your world through your words, body language, and spirit. If each of us put positive purpose behind our words, what a better world we all would live in! Remember, we are here to solve life's problems. We have the ability to find solutions as well as the key to open up a new world of understanding. That key is communication. Command your world and win!

About The Author

Dr. Bonnie Winfrey is the CEO of Kailen & Kyler Enterprises. She began her communications career over thirty years ago. Dr. Winfrey is a media and public relations executive, marketing consultant, a freelance newspaper reporter, and an award-winning producer/director. She's well versed in corporate communication issues and.has trained thousands of executives and professionals in communication etiquette.

During her career, she's worked for The American Broadcasting Company (WLS-TV Chicago), CNN Headline News (Atlanta, GA), The Weather Channel (Atlanta, GA), and FOX Broadcasting (Chicago). She has written for both print (Herald News, Chicago Sun-Times, and Chicago Tribune) and broadcast media. She has also hosted several televion shows. For two years, she was the host of Community Connection, an AT&T Broadband/Comcast broadcast. Today, she is the host of "In the Know with Bonnie Winfrey."

As a communication and media strategist, Dr. Winfrey coaches individuals and businesses on how to build their brand and perfect their presence in the business and media world.

Dr. Bonnie Winfrey holds a bachelor of arts degree in Mass Media Communications with honors recognition from the University of Illinois at Chicago. She is also a graduate of the Barbizon School of Modeling in Chicago. Dr. Winfrey was awarded an honorary degree of Doctorate of Communications from the Thessalonika A. Embry University.

Dr. Winfrey has also received specialized training in the area of voice and coaching from the Judith Sullivan School of Voice in Atlanta, GA. She received certification through Les Brown and James Dentley's "Inspired 2Speak Program." Her knowledge and experience coupled with her desire to strive for excellence has launched her to become a giant in the communications industry. She has received many awards including five national "Telly Awards" for documentary and corporate video productions, a "Summit Award," "The Communicator's Award", two "Videographer Awards," and was a finalist for the 13th Black Harvest International Festival of Film, Video and TV (Gene Siskel Film Center) for her documentary entitled *Katherine Dunham: Rhythm & Motion, The Never Ending Dance*. She was also honored to be chosen as a two-time judge for the Emmys.

Dr. Winfrey serves the community in many capacities. She's a community advisor for Dow Chemical Company. She is also a trustee for Silver Cross Hospital, New Lenox, Illinois; Public Relations chair and second Vice President of the Zonta Club of Joliet; and an advisor to the Joliet Historic Museum. Dr. Winfrey has been a board advisor for the Easter Seals Rehabilitation Center for Will and Grundy Counties. For two years, she served as chairman of the board and chief volunteer officer for Easter Seals, and she served on the board of directors for six years. She also produced and hosted the Easter Seals telethon pre-show since its inception for over twenty years and has been a regular host on the actual telethon.

Dr. Winfrey was a former judge and contestants interview coach for the Illinois Junior Miss Scholarship Program. She has also had the honor of judging the 2002 Ms. Illinois American United States Pageant and has had the opportunity to be an interview coach for participants for the Mrs. Illinois International Pageant 2004, as well as a judge for the 2004 Indiana Junior Miss Scholarship Program.

Dr. Winfrey is married to Dr. Keith Winfrey for thirty-seven years and they have two sons, Kailen and Kyler.

"Communication is the key to opening a whole world of understanding."
